Palgrave Studies in the History of Finance

Series Editors
D'Maris Coffman
Bartlett Faculty of Built Environment
University College London
London, UK

Tony K. Moore
ICMA Centre, Henley Business School
University of Reading
Reading, UK

Martin Allen
Department of Coins and Medals,
Fitzwilliam Museum
University of Cambridge
Cambridge, UK

Sophus Reinert
Harvard Business School
Cambridge, MA, USA

The study of the history of financial institutions, markets, instruments and concepts is vital if we are to understand the role played by finance today. At the same time, the methodologies developed by finance academics can provide a new perspective for historical studies. Palgrave Studies in the History of Finance is a multi-disciplinary effort to emphasise the role played by finance in the past, and what lessons historical experiences have for us. It presents original research, in both authored monographs and edited collections, from historians, finance academics and economists, as well as financial practitioners.

More information about this series at
http://www.palgrave.com/gp/series/14583

Aaron Graham

Bills of Union

Money, Empire and Ambitions
in the Mid-Eighteenth Century British Atlantic

Aaron Graham
Faculty of History
University of Oxford
Oxford, UK

ISSN 2662-5164   ISSN 2662-5172   (electronic)
Palgrave Studies in the History of Finance
ISBN 978-3-030-67676-6   ISBN 978-3-030-67677-3   (eBook)
https://doi.org/10.1007/978-3-030-67677-3

© The Editor(s) (if applicable) and The Author(s), under exclusive licence to Springer Nature Switzerland AG 2021
This work is subject to copyright. All rights are solely and exclusively licensed by the Publisher, whether the whole or part of the material is concerned, specifically the rights of translation, reprinting, reuse of illustrations, recitation, broadcasting, reproduction on microfilms or in any other physical way, and transmission or information storage and retrieval, electronic adaptation, computer software, or by similar or dissimilar methodology now known or hereafter developed.
The use of general descriptive names, registered names, trademarks, service marks, etc. in this publication does not imply, even in the absence of a specific statement, that such names are exempt from the relevant protective laws and regulations and therefore free for general use.
The publisher, the authors and the editors are safe to assume that the advice and information in this book are believed to be true and accurate at the date of publication. Neither the publisher nor the authors or the editors give a warranty, expressed or implied, with respect to the material contained herein or for any errors or omissions that may have been made. The publisher remains neutral with regard to jurisdictional claims in published maps and institutional affiliations.

This Palgrave Pivot imprint is published by the registered company Springer Nature Switzerland AG.
The registered company address is: Gewerbestrasse 11, 6330 Cham, Switzerland

Preface

This book began as a footnote. Working on corruption, government, finance and state formation in British America between 1754 and 1783, I became interested by the number of projects for monetary unions and continental currencies, and the hypotheticals and counterfactuals they suggested. Initially it seemed like a footnote would be sufficient to explain these curiosities, but as I continued to find more plans it became clear that there was also more to be said. The footnote thus became a paragraph and then an article, and now, finally, nearly eight years later, a book.

In the course of those eight years I have benefited enormously from the help, advice and assistance of a large number of people. I would like to thank in particular Stephen Conway, Julian Hoppit, Trevor Burnard and Matthew Dziennik for their conversations on all matters imperial and economic. I have also profited from speaking with Robert Wright, Ronald Michener, Katherine Smoak and Andrew Edwards on matters financial. Matthew and Andrew also kindly gave up their time in the midst of a pandemic to read through the draft chapters and offer their thoughts. Earlier drafts were much improved by the feedback offered at the 'Capitalism and Revolution' workshop in Birmingham in May 2019, and the reviewers at the *William and Mary Quarterly*. Many others, too numerous to name, have also assisted.

Much of the early research and writing was carried out during a British Academy Postdoctoral Fellowship at the University of Oxford, and was continued during an Early Career Fellowship at University College London funded by the Leverhulme Trust. I am grateful to both bodies for their support. The William L. Clements Library awarded me an Earhart Foundation Fellowship in America History in 2013, and the Henry E. Huntington Library an Andrew M. Mellon Foundation Fellowship in the same year, and I am indebted to both for their generous assistance, which allowed me to consult many of the records discussed in this book.

This work has also relied on the aid of the staff at libraries and archives on both sides of the Atlantic, including the British Library, the National Archives of the United Kingdom, the Bodleian Library, the William L. Clements Library and the Henry E. Huntington Library. The Newbery Library and the John Rylands Library helpfully sent me copies of material relating to Sir Alexander Cuming, while the Bibliothèque Nationale de France was able to digitise their copy of his *Case* for me. The proposal by Charles Williamos in the appendices is reproduced with the kind permission of the Trustees of the Dartmouth Heirloom Trust.

At Palgrave, Ruth Noble and Tula Weis have been enormously helpful and made the process as painless as possible, and I am grateful to them both.

Finally, this could not have been done without the support and encouragement of my friends and family. Hanaan Marwah, Ioanna Tsakiropoulou and Anne Hanley have always been there, in the best possible way, as have Josh, Emma and my wider family. My deepest debts though are still to my parents, Robert and Sharon Graham. So it is once more to them that I dedicate this book, with renewed and even more profound love, affection and gratitude, and also once again to the memories of my grandparents, Gus and Betty Graham and Arlene and Monty Hambury, whom I hope would have been very proud to see it.

Oxford, UK   Aaron Graham

Contents

1	Introduction	1
2	Land Banks	27
3	Specie Banks	47
4	Conclusion	77

Appendix A: Sir Alexander Cuming, Commonplace Book (Circa 1764 to 1767) — 101

Appendix B: Lauchlin Macleane to the Earl of Hertford 'Proposal' (1765) — 105

Appendix C: Charles Williamos 'Plan for Establishing a Bank in North America' (c. 1766) — 111

Appendix D: 'Proposals for Establishing Paper Currency in North America' (Undated but c. 1767) — 119

Bibliography — 123

Index — 139

ABBREVIATIONS

BL   British Library, London
CL   William L. Clements Library, Ann Arbor, Michigan
HL   Henry E. Huntington Library, San Marino, California
JRL   The John Rylands Library, Manchester
LBGA Lloyds Banking Group Archives, London
NL   The Newberry Library, Chicago, Illinois
ODNB Oxford Dictionary of National Biography
SRO   Staffordshire Record Office, Stafford
TNA   The National Archives of the United Kingdom, London

CHAPTER 1

Introduction

Abstract The key themes of this chapter are money, empire and ambition in the British Atlantic in the eighteenth century. Shortages of circulating medium affected not only the colonial economy but also imperial warfare and revenues, leading to a range of monetary expedients. As imperial territories in North America and the Caribbean expanded, especially in the wake of the Seven Years War (1756–1763), the British Empire was increasingly seen as a cohesive and coherent unit, requiring correspondingly ambitious and uniform strategic and commercial policies. The problems and inconveniences caused by absence of a common circulating medium became increasingly glaring, and lay behind the growing number of proposals for colonial monetary union and the creation of an imperial paper currency.

Keywords Currency • Money • Finance • Banking • Empire • Reform • Monetary union

The eighteenth century saw many financial experiments as Britons and Americans tried to work out how to manage paper currency and banking in the British Atlantic. Previous studies have looked at the successes and failures of schemes in individual colonies. But some had grander ambitions, such as Benjamin Franklin, and offered proposals for 'imperial' paper currencies which would circulate more broadly and help knit together the empire in North America and the West Indies, especially in the wake of the Seven Years War between 1756 and 1763. So far these proposals for monetary unions have either been overlooked or treated as curiosities, because they are scattered across multiple archives on both sides of the Atlantic and never came to fruition. Yet examining them together shows, firstly, the range of monetary and financial thought in the region during this period, helping to restate the place of the British Atlantic in these debates and its participation in a wider 'empire of credit'. Secondly, it reveals a key but understudied aspect of the programme for imperial reform which gathered pace between the 1740s and 1760s, in particular the growing perception on both sides of the Atlantic of British colonial territories as parts of a financial and monetary—as well as political, economic, strategic—whole. Thirdly, it provides a context for understanding the subsequent pursuit of monetary union by both the United States and the British Empire after 1775, as further iterations of efforts to address issues first encountered in the mid-eighteenth century, using solutions also pioneered in that period. This chapter introduces the key themes of the volume and presents an overview of money, empire and ambitions in the British Atlantic. The next two chapters examine the proposals offered, covering land banks and 'specie' banks, respectively. Finally, the conclusion draws these elements together to reflect on projects for monetary unions and the broader processes of imperial reform, nation-building and state formation that lay behind them.

Money

The British Atlantic in the eighteenth century was marked by perennial and pervasive shortages of currency and credit.[1] Much to the disappointment of early settlers there were no gold or silver mines to be found, and Britain banned the export of its own coinage, so the colonies had no choice but to look elsewhere for a means of exchange.[2] Heavy use was made of barter and book credit, which allowed the mutual offsetting of debts, and the bills of exchange, bonds and promissory notes issued by individuals had a wide circulation. Colonists also relied on the foreign coins they acquired by trade, directly with Spanish and Portuguese America or by exchanges between the continental and the Caribbean colonies. Many coins were underweight or counterfeit, but nevertheless quickly drained away to Europe. To pay for the manufactures and the slaves supplied by British merchants, colonists could send produce for sale in Britain and Europe or bills of exchange drawn on that produce, but in the last resort silver or gold specie had to be paid, cutting down the colonial money supply. Colonial monetary policy was therefore an aspect of wider imperial finance and commerce, part of the 'empire of credit' which helped to stitch together the British Atlantic world throughout the eighteenth century.[3] It was generally addressed, however, in a piecemeal fashion, which then created a number of problems as reformers began to contemplate imperial integration.

The colonies of the British Atlantic experimented with a wide variety of measures, some of which will be discussed in more detail in the following chapters, to try to address the issue of money. A mint operated in Massachusetts between 1652 and 1682 until it was suppressed as an insupportable affront to the royal prerogative.[4] In its absence provinces tinkered with the ratings or formal valuations put on foreign coins, either deliberately to attract the coins into circulation or, as recent work has suggested, to recognise the higher rates that they already carried among merchants in the market.[5] Colonists showed a higher tolerance for clipped and counterfeit coins, which helped to keep them in circulation.[6] Acts in Virginia and Maryland in 1730 and 1747 respectively provided for the emission of 'tobacco notes', a paper money backed by tobacco of specified quality deposited in a government warehouse and exchangeable for the note at a fixed price.[7] Every province also eventually issued their own paper money, starting with Massachusetts in 1690. In a process that James Ferguson defined as 'currency finance', bills of credit secured on future tax receipts were issued to serve as paper money, circulating until the notes expired and were recalled or redeemed.[8] Most colonies also set up loan offices or land banks in the eighteenth century, emitting paper money backed by private mortgages. Farmers or planters wishing to borrow money mortgaged their land to the loan office trustees and received their loan in paper money, which, until 1764, was sometimes made a legal tender for all public and private debts.[9] Experiments were made at several points of private banks that resembled the country banks of England and Ireland, issuing notes secured on the deposits of coin and other colonial securities.[10] These provided colonists with some of the circulating medium they required.

By issuing notes upon the security of land or taxes, through the loan office and the currency finance system, colonies could also address the pressing shortage of credit for agricultural, commercial and industrial development noted above. As frontier territories, by and large, the colonies faced heavy initial costs, for clearing and working land and for developing infrastructure to enable this produce to be moved for processing and export.[11] Costs were highest in the most profitable colonies, the Southern and Caribbean plantation economies, where the cultivation of sugar, coffee, cotton, indigo and tobacco required heavier initial investments in land, slaves and industrial apparatus.[12] Most planters depended on credit supplied by merchants in London, Bristol, Liverpool and Glasgow, in the form of slaves and British manufactures sold on long credits of up to two years. There were many disadvantages for colonists in this process. Credit was advanced upon British terms and subject to British demands, with some merchants demanding high rates of interest, or using their leverage over planters to demand the exclusive rights to consignments of sugar and tobacco, forcing down the price. Moreover, credit crises in Britain could force merchants to curtail lending and call in colonial debts, as in 1763 and 1772, withdrawing credit at a time when the drain of specie from colonial economies was usually accelerating.[13] As a result, many colonists were eager to find domestic sources of credit from local capitalists and institutions, and the emission of notes by colonial assemblies promised to make this even more generally available.[14]

Each province and colony therefore developed its own currency policies to address the shortage of specie, broadly in line with others but subject to local circumstances and interests, and with barely any imperial regulation to impose uniformity, colonial currencies fluctuated against each other unpredictably as a result. For instance, the formal rate or 'par' of exchange between New York and Pennsylvania currencies by 1763 was 6.66 per cent, since New York rated the dollar at 8s and Pennsylvania at 7s 6d, which equalled a rate of exchange on London of £177.77 New York currency and £166.67 Pennsylvania currency per £100 sterling.[15] However, factors such as the volume of trade, the demand for bills and money, the amount of paper issued by each colony and its circulation between them, all meant that the actual rate of exchange between New York and Philadelphia, and on London, moved up and down within the band set by more stable factors such as the intrinsic and face prices of foreign gold and silver coins. Since colonies were unable, and the imperial government in general unwilling, to intervene directly to limit or regulate colonial paper emissions, over-issue by one colony could have effects not only upon its own colonists and their creditors but also on neighbouring ones in which their bills circulated. For example, Rhode Island wrecked the circulation of paper money in New England in the 1740s by over-issuing paper notes, which also circulated in the rest of New England and were widely thought to have caused runaway inflation.[16] This directly resulted in the imperial Currency Act of 1751, by which Parliament banned the issue of all legal tender bills of credit by the colonies in New England and required them to redeem their outstanding issues to correct this devaluation.

This episode hinted at the destructive potential of the currency system, which not only resulted in a disordered mass of fluctuating currencies as colonies tinkered with paper money but also threatened the property of British investors. Provinces besides as Rhode Island might deliberately issue money which they had no means to back, either because they expected that the economic growth it produced would provide the means or because the devaluation it produced relative to sterling helped to push down the real value of colonial debts to British creditors. The issue of whether or not this was actually happening in the eighteenth century has given rise to a contentious and occasionally ill-tempered historiographical debate about the amount of money in British America and its velocity, and whether this is sufficient to explain the clear variations in colonial exchange rates. Joseph Ernst, Bruce Smith, Robert West and most recently Farley Grubb have argued that the use of paper money was widespread and was generally useful, and that changes in quantity arising from over-issue had little or no effect upon prices and rates of exchange, apart perhaps in New England before 1750.[17] Variations instead reflected a range of other factors, such as the imbalances of trade and the availability of credit, or the credibility of the backing that bills of credit had. By contrast, Ronald Michener and Robert Wright have revised the earlier, simpler applications of 'quantity theory' developed by Curtis Nettels, Leslie Brock and others to argue that as the specie was displaced from general circulation by paper money lacking adequate backing, as in New England or South Carolina, prices and the rates of exchange increased.[18] Only when paper issues were small relative to the size of the economy—and cushioned by an adequate specie buffer, as in Pennsylvania and New York—did the emission of paper money fail to cause substantial depreciation.[19]

The outcome of this debate is less important for the purposes of this book than the fact that it mirrors a controversy which contemporaries in the eighteenth century endlessly rehashed, and which shaped their views. As successive studies have shown, there was a strong body of opinion in British America from the seventeenth century which praised the issuing, even over-issuing, of paper money for its ability to stimulate economic growth and reduce the cost of imports.[20] There was an equally strong body of opinion on both sides of the British Atlantic which argued that paper money issues inevitably caused devaluation, commercial instability and economic disruption, and that the only solution was either a specie currency or a paper one closely tied to it.[21] Each side could point to a well-established body of theoretical literature, and to specific examples. The Currency Acts of 1751 and 1764 were a product of the ascendancy of imperial and colonial interest groups who persuaded the Crown that colonists in Rhode Island and Virginia, respectively, were deliberately flooding the region with paper money to avoid paying their debts to their British creditors.[22] The Currency Act of 1751 banned the emission of legal tender paper money by colonies in New England; its successor in 1764 extended this to the rest of British America and encompassed non-legal tender paper too, but also permitted it to be issued with royal permission. It soon proved so inconvenient that a series of exceptions developed, culminating in the Currency Act of 1773, which allowed paper money to be issued as long as it was securely backed and not a legal tender.[23] A similar concern about the inflationary effects of excessive paper money in Scotland led to the Scottish Banking Act the following year in 1765.[24] This prohibited banks from issuing paper money whose redemption in specie was 'at the option' of the banks rather than the bearer, and in denominations below £1, both measures likewise thought to encourage paper note over-issue and financial instability. A number of practices, precedents and perceptions therefore shaped how the various interests in the British Atlantic began to consider the state of imperial and colonial money and finance between 1748 and 1768.

Ambitions

Moreover, it is necessary to see the various proposals for an imperial or continental currency which emerged around this time as the solutions to a set of problems which had existed in the past but not to the same extent, and had now become pressing issues because they were now at odds with new and developing ambitions for empire. Those ambitions were less tolerant of incoherence and inconsistency, and increasingly saw the British Empire as a unified political, strategic and economic entity acting for the support of the metropole. In one sense such visions were nothing new. They were implicit in the assumptions of seventeenth-century mercantilism, which saw metropolitan and colonial territories as complementary parts of a complete and largely self-contained economic system. The creation of the Dominion of New England between 1686 and 1688 had been an early attempt to impose a degree of political unity and central control over British America, and several other plans emerged during the active phase of British imperial governance between 1680 and 1720, and again in later years.[25] Most notoriously, Benjamin Franklin submitted a plan for a colonial union to the Albany conference in 1754, organised along similar lines.[26] The visions of imperial unity which began to assert themselves after 1764 were of the same type, but also took account of the vastly increased scope of empire, which now included Canada, Illinois, the Floridas and the Ceded Islands in the Caribbean, and had the potential for an even wider range of economic, strategic, military, fiscal and financial unities. 'At the heart of this new vision', Max Edelson argues, moreover, 'was a working philosophy of empire … that aimed to connect far-flung sites of occupation through the integrative power of commerce' and the fiscal and military organs of the imperial state.[27] The lack of an imperial monetary instrument capable of supporting and promoting these three elements—commerce, revenue and defence—began to appear to some writers an important deficit.

In fiscal and military terms, for instance, imperial policy after 1764 began to show a broader strategic vision. Whereas diplomatic relations with the Native Americans had hitherto been the responsibility of individual colonies, they were now to be in the hands of two Superintendents of Indian Affairs appointed by the British government, who would help to formulate policy.[28] The western lands beyond the Appalachians were declared closed to European settlement by the proclamation of 1763, and the British government despatched surveying parties to negotiate, fix and map the line of demarcation. At least 10,000 troops were to be permanently stationed on the continent, to defend the frontiers against French or Spanish revanchism. The aim was not, at least in 1763, to use the army to impose imperial policy on the colonists or to act as a police force, though it soon moved into both roles.[29] The naval squadron in British America was expanded, both for defence and to help enforce customs and navigation laws.[30] All this was to be paid for by individual colonial contributions, as in the past, but also by a new series of imperial taxes laid evenly across British America, including the British Caribbean. The Stamp Act of 1765 reflected this new vision of imperial fiscal-military unity, as did the Townshend Acts of 1767 and 1768 which replaced it.[31] To help develop and enforce this uniform customs policy the Vice-Admiralty courts were overhauled, and an American Board of Customs was created in 1767, along with an Inspector-General of Imports and Exports to collect statistical data.[32] Imperial policy therefore embodied a new and expansive strategic vision after 1764, aimed at the creation of a uniform system of imperial fiscal and military administration that depended, as will become clear, on frictionless transatlantic and intercolonial flows of money.

These plans overlapped with the determination of the Board of Trade to force the pace of colonial development in order to reinforce the commercial unity of empire. There were long-standing concerns from the powerful West India interest before 1764 about smuggling within the closed mercantilist system, as American merchants transported provisions and timber to the British Caribbean, took their profits as coin or bills, and then exchanged them in foreign colonies such as Saint Domingue for cheaper molasses and rum, contributing to the leakage of coin outside the empire and thus the shortage of specie in British America.[33] The rapid development of the Floridas and Ceded Islands with imperial support would meet the needs of American consumers and cut off this trade, complementing the penalties created by the Sugar Act of 1764 and the measures against smugglers noted above.[34] In practical terms this represented an extension of methods first developed for the settlement of the ceded portions of St Kitts after 1713, and perfected most recently at a provincial level by the formal settlement of Georgia in 1733 and Nova Scotia in 1749. Other proposals circulated for settling the Illinois and Canada.[35] More substantively, free ports were created after 1766 in Jamaica, Dominica and other Caribbean territories for enabling trade with Spanish America.[36] As recent work has emphasised, this was ultimately intended to support the mercantilist system and the economic unity of empire, by allowing the export of slaves and British manufactures in return for gold and silver, provisions and other essentials, a regulated set of exchanges that would undercut smuggling. The empire was thus increasingly seen as an economic whole, once again based on seamless financial and monetary integration.

The plans by the Board of Trade, expressed most clearly in 1763 in their 'Report on acquisitions in America', therefore reflected a coherent vision of empire that was shared in its essentials, if not in exact details, by a wider public in the British Atlantic. 'Britain imagined America anew', Edelson has concluded, 'by seeing its collection of mainland colonies as a single space at the centre of a reformed imperial system', in which the imperial state would create the conditions for development.[37] Imperial forces would police the new territory and prevent smuggling and disorder, carrying on the surveying and mapping that would allow ordered, systematic and rational settlement of undeveloped territories. In some cases this complemented colonial plans for development, as evidenced by the tidal waves of investment which soon flooded into the Ceded Islands to profit from this new sugar frontier.[38] In several other cases it cut against them, as demonstrated by the difficulties settling lands opened up in East Florida and preventing colonists crossing the Proclamation Line into Indian territory, as well as their repeated efforts to secure looser monetary policies in order to provide the credit for this expansion. In every instance it was expected that the imperial state would intervene, by deploying troops funded at least in part by imperial taxes, making the effectiveness of the imperial state a key element in these ambitious economic objectives. The plans for a continental or imperial currency which emerged were either a direct reaction to this burgeoning interest in imperial unity after 1764 or a response to the problems which were increasingly arising from putting it into effect, or even sometimes both.

Empire

The established problem of colonial monetary shortfalls and the new and growing problem of imperial commercial, fiscal and military integration therefore came together in the mid-eighteenth century to highlight the limitations of the *status quo*. In theory a common imperial currency was provided by the Spanish silver dollar, which was accepted throughout the British Atlantic at the rates specified by law in each colony. However, not only were dollars frequently scarce, due to both a lack of supply and the tendency to export them to Britain to settle debts, but they also carried differing values depending on their weight and scarcity. For example, they had a market value of 4s 6d sterling in Britain, close to their intrinsic value in silver at its market price of 5s 2d per ounce, but were worth up to 5s sterling in Nova Scotia, where they were much scarcer.[39] A merchant seeking to send money from New York to Halifax to purchase goods or supply the imperial garrison therefore had to take account of the respective pars of exchange, the market price of dollars, their intrinsic weight (including losses from clipping or wear and tear) and the market price of silver, and then consider whether this was cheaper than sending a bill of exchange, whose prices likewise fluctuated depending on the reputation of the drawee, the period of maturity or 'usance', the market for bills and a range of other factors.

This posed problems, for a start, in economic terms. Although it remained the case that most colonies had a closer commercial relationship with the British Isles than they did with each other, the economic connections between them were strengthening. The British Caribbean was dependent on the provisions and timber shipped from British North America, for instance, which relied in turn upon the coin and molasses or rum shipped back in return.[40] Similar commercial relations existed with the southern colonies in return for tobacco and rice. Trading connections spanned individual colonies, and the circulation of paper notes outside their home colonies reflected not only the pressing shortages of circulating medium but also, to some extent, the growing volume of intercolonial economic exchange. Pennsylvania paper money circulated throughout the Virginia backcountry, for instance, and New Jersey currency enjoyed a premium because it could be used by New York merchants to settle debts in Philadelphia and vice versa, while New England was a unified currency zone before 1751, hence the disruption caused by Rhode Island.[41] Yet the process was fraught with uncertainty. Provincial paper carried no legal value outside its home colony and its value in the market therefore varied based upon the ebbs and flows of commercial opinion, including the amount issued, its backing and the overall imbalance of intercolonial and -imperial trade. As future chapters will show, this state of affairs was felt to be inconvenient, expensive and inconsistent with the economic unity of the British imperial system, now coming into focus after 1764.

These problems were also felt by those concerned in military finance. Although the Seven Years War began in the Illinois in 1754, within two years there were extensive contingents of British and provincial troops in the Great Lakes and in Canada, and other expeditions were mounted to the Pennsylvania and South Carolina backcountry and even further afield to the Caribbean. Each place had different legal ratings and market values for foreign coins, and paying the troops was an administrative nightmare as a result.[42] Dollars were hard to come by, and on occasion, it was found necessary for troops to be paid in the paper money issued by New York or Pennsylvania.[43] Even when sufficient coin could be found, either by shipping it out from Britain or by raising it locally, the fluctuating market rates meant the troops and the public either enjoyed large profits or heavy losses. These problems led William Johnston, the deputy-paymaster in New York, to suggest to the commander-in-chief Lord Loudon in August 1756 that dollars be paid over to troops across North America at the New York rate of 4s 8d sterling per dollar, regardless of their weight, and other foreign coins in proportion.[44] This would simplify bookkeeping and the process of paying over the specie, since it would be unnecessary to weigh it and calculate its market value. It risked cheating the troops though by issuing them with underweight coin, and meant that troops in northern colonies might profit by selling their dollars to merchants at 5s sterling, while those in the southern colonies, where underweight coins went for as little as 4s 2d sterling, might lose by the same amount. The agent to the contractors for supplying the army in North America with money therefore opposed the suggestion, adding that he thought it would be impossible in any case to secure enough dollars to make it work.

The inevitable result of this system, especially faced with such contradictory aims—administrative clarity and convenience, financial economy and strategic flexibility—was chaos and confusion. Johnston and the agent, John Hunter, each accused the other of corruption and fraud, and these issues were fought out again in Britain at the Treasury between Johnston, Loudon and the contractors. 'Unless an Act of Parliament passes to fix invariably the rates at which gold and silver coins shall pass at alike through the whole continent', they wrote, moving troops between provinces would confuse all accounting measures, while a single rate would lead to profiteering and exhaust provinces of their specie.[45] As I have shown elsewhere, the conflict represented the difference of perspective between an official in a single province, the centre of the war effort, and a set of contractors whose commercial and financial obligations covered the whole of British America; there was no 'right' answer, merely a judgement as to which set of priorities were to be favoured over the others.[46] Eventually the Treasury followed Johnston's suggestion and fixed the value of the dollar paid over to troops at 4s 8d sterling, regardless of its value in either America or Britain. This system of 'army sterling' provided simplicity and clarity during the American Revolutionary War, with the Treasury following the same practice of hiring contractors to remit cash or raise it locally, and persisted after 1783 as British imperial forces moved further overseas to Asia and Australia.[47] In 1825 it was junked and replaced with an equally arbitrary and inflexible standard of 4s 4d during the programme of imperial monetary standardisation described in the final chapter.[48] The growing military and strategic unity of empire therefore created a pressure by 1764 for a uniform imperial currency, rather than a mass of colonial ones.

Similar problems faced the collectors of imperial revenues, which were levied in sterling and were no less vulnerable than private sterling debts to the fluctuation and complexities of colonial currencies. The quit-rents payable upon Crown land grants had long been a source of great contention for precisely this reason, with receivers for the British Crown and provincial proprietors repeatedly protesting about being required to accept payment in devalued paper or coin which did not carry its full sterling value when remitted home.[49] The solution adopted by both the Stamp Act in 1765 and the Revenue Act which replaced it in 1767 was to stipulate that payments were not to be made in colonial paper or even by foreign coins by their rated value, since colonial assemblies might be tempted to fiddle with the ratings to defraud the system. Instead, silver coins would only be taken by weight at 5s 6d per ounce, its market price in London, despite the clear lack of coins in circulation for payment. As Andrew Edwards has recently suggested, American resistance to the Stamp Act thus partly reflected a resentment at these unrealistic demands to be paid in coins that did not exist there.[50] 'American colonists opposed the taxes because they appeared impossible to pay', he notes, 'and they could not avoid paying them without abandoning many of the protections of British law', since without such payments the legal system ground to a halt.[51] In fact, the situation was even more serious than he suggests. Because so much of the specie circulating in British America was underweight or counterfeit and retained its legal value because it nevertheless passed at par, even those with silver coin would have to pay it over at much less than its legal value, at further loss to themselves.[52]

Both the imperial military and imperial revenue service had therefore adopted by 1764 a series of messy, inconsistent and highly unsatisfactory expedients in the face of what was, as far as several officials in the British government were concerned, a messy, inconsistent and highly unsatisfactory system of colonial currencies. This sentiment was hardly novel. Following a landmark assay of foreign coins by the Mint in 1702, a royal proclamation was issued in 1704 fixing the maximum rates at which specified coins could circulate within the British Atlantic.[53] The dollar was to pass at 4s 6d sterling, for instance, and no more than 6s currency. However, it was widely ignored, even after being embodied in a parliamentary act of 1708, and although New England and the Southern colonies were eventually brought into conformity and fixed a ceiling of 6s currency upon the dollar or 'proclamation money', this did not stop continued tinkering, especially among the mid-Atlantic colonies. Passed as part of the wider initiative between 1680 and 1720 to tighten up and unify imperial administration, defence, revenue and commerce, the subsequent period of 'salutary neglect' meant that the 1708 Act became a dead letter.[54] Action was taken against specific problems, such as the extension of a ban on corporate banking in 1741 in response to the creation of the Massachusetts banks, but it was largely piecemeal and reactive, and failed to address the underlying issues. As Ernst, Sosin, Brock and others have noted, the Currency Acts of 1751 and 1764 were the first efforts made since 1708 to develop and impose a uniform imperial currency policy, and although they were intended primarily to address the problems of over-issues noted above, they would have served a secondary purpose of reducing the fluctuations between the colonial currencies resulting from such over-issues.[55] Others, however, hoped to grasp the nettle and to adopt measures which would address this issue directly and provide a new paper currency suitable for the growing scale of British imperial rule.

In developing these plans the projectors lacked obvious precedents, and this book will show how they drew from a wide range of financial and monetary theories and practice and ended up with a wide range of solutions. The general familiarity in British America with paper notes issued by either colonial banks or governments, and backed by land, coin or taxation, presented obvious precedents which could be scaled up as necessary. There was at least one precedent available for a monetary union, the alignments of English and Scottish currency in 1604 after the union of the crowns, which fixed a rate of exchange between the respective currencies and agreed common standards of fineness and weight for coins legal in both kingdoms.[56] At the Union in 1707 the Scottish coins in circulation were called in and recoined at this common standard to make up for the debasement which the coinage had undergone in the late seventeenth century at the Scottish mint. Other precedents were the widespread circulation of Bank of England notes within the Britain Isles after 1694, as well as the general circulation of colonial paper notes outside their respective colonies. Behind a number of proposals lay monetary theory, including the conflicts noted above between supporters of 'hard money' backed by the intrinsic value of the metal, either circulating directly or as notes convertible into coin on demand, and the supporters of 'soft money', who were willing to accept other forms of collateral, including land, commodities, government and corporate securities and even, in extremis, the public faith and the promise of a note being legal tender. Seeking to address the problems of imperial unity, the plans for an imperial currency were in dialogue with these practices, but produced a range of different answers which reflected the precedents they adopted, the conditions on the ground and the change that they wished to see in the British Atlantic world.

Consequences

At one level all of these plans were ultimately a dead end. None were adopted by the British government, though a few came close, and after 1768 no further plans were submitted. The unwieldy expedients of 'army sterling' and customs currency were carried over into the American Revolutionary War and the post-war empire. When the first continental or supra-colonial currency began to appear in America in 1775, it was issued by the Continental Congress, which embarked upon a large-scale programme of currency finance by issuing notes backed by the promise of revenue contributions by individual states under the Articles of Confederation and, in the final analysis, by the public faith.[57] The value of looking at the early proposals for a continental currency is nevertheless threefold.[58]

Firstly, examining these proposals shows the range of monetary and financial thought in circulation in the British Atlantic during this period, and thus the origins of the process of monetary union in the post-1783 United States and the British Empire. A similar approach has been used to understand the earliest stages of the British 'financial revolution', during the late seventeenth century. Carl Wennerlind has most recently demonstrated that it was only in the 1650s that paper money first became possible in England, after the intellectual circles around Samuel Hartlib exploited alchemical theory to explain how the value of gold or land might be transmuted into the printed paper which represented it.[59] Once this was accepted and extended with new principles of probabilistic reasoning that could make sense of credit, trust and reputation, political economists could design financial institutions to promote all three; 'the conceptualisation of a new financial architecture and the grounds for its general acceptance', Wennerlind concludes, 'would not have been possible without an earlier revolution in political economy ... [and] how people conceived of credit'.[60] Along with the example of successful banks such as the Amsterdam Wisselbank, the circulation of these treaties and proposals helped to introduce concepts of paper money to the wider public, and impossible ideas such as a national bank began to move into the political and economic mainstream in Britain and America.[61] Studies of similar episodes of financial projects, such as the failed schemes for a Bank of Ireland in 1721 and

1733 and for the Land Bank and Silver Bank in Massachusetts in 1740, have been equally fruitful.[62] The many plans for an imperial paper currency after 1748, though never enacted, therefore reveal how the intellectual foundations of an 'empire of credit' in the British Atlantic were laid.

Secondly, the proposals for an imperial paper currency demonstrate the financial and monetary components of the movement for British imperial reform during the mid-eighteenth century. As this chapter has shown, recent work has noted the increasing unity and cohesion of this world in the mid-eighteenth century, seen in the efforts to enact uniform commercial, fiscal and military policies. The Currency Acts of 1708, 1751, 1764 and 1773, although operating only at the level of individual colonies, exemplified this movement through their efforts to impose a uniform currency policy upon the region, contributing to its stability and cohesion. The plans studied here went further and considered what a common continental or imperial currency could achieve, in political and economic terms, by bolstering either colonial commerce or imperial authority, or sometimes both. They drew upon sets of assumptions about the nature of money and credit, the role of currency and banks and the purpose of empire which were found to varying degrees in groups on both sides of the Atlantic. Ultimately, they strengthen recent findings on the scope and scale of popular ambitions for empire in the mid-eighteenth century at the moment when it was reaching a point of fracture.

Thirdly, the proposals likewise indicate the context for later attempts at monetary reform within the United States and the British Empire. The creation of the Continental dollar in 1775 created a common unit of account for the territories in rebellion which supplemented rather than superseded the units used by each colony, while the paper currency itself also provided a common medium of exchange. In effect it was an imperial currency, designed to address many of the same military, fiscal, financial and economic problems first identified in the 1740s, and faced similar problems, since individual states continued to issue their own notes, denominated either in dollars or in the local unit of account. This loose monetary union was tightened up after 1787 in the new Constitution, which banned the emission of state currencies and established a fixed rate of conversion between the new federal dollar and gold and silver coins, reviving the common standard previously supplied by British sterling. However, although the United States Mint began to strike gold and silver coins on this new standard, foreign coins also continued to circulate; the only common units of exchange were the paper notes and instruments issued by the federal treasury, by the first and second Bank of the United States, and by private banks. It was not until 1865 that the United States even began to move towards a full monetary union based on a single uniform medium of exchange, the United States notes. The colonial proposals for a single unit of account and medium of exchange for British America were therefore the first of repeated attempts which reflected the workings of similar dynamics.

The departure of the Thirteen Colonies in 1783 also left numerous colonies in both the British Caribbean and what would become known as British North America, which continued to expand in size and complexity. Issues of currency were submerged rather than resolved, and resurfaced in the 1820s as the Colonial Office and imperial officials embarked on quixotic efforts to impose a bare degree of standardisation and uniformity upon a vast and sprawling empire, and which laid the foundations for the emergence of sterling as a world currency after 1870.[63] The variation of currency was one of the issues they took up, through the proclamation in 1825 noted above. In practice it met with only a moderate degree of success in the British Caribbean and Australia, and none at all in British North America and South Asia, but it reflected a continuation of the same concerns, for imperial administration and colonial development, which lay behind the proposals of the 1760s. Similar pressures lay behind related measures such as the development between 1825 and 1846 of regulations for the new imperial joint-stock banks, in an effort to control the irresponsible emission of paper money by private interests.[64] The problems and solutions of finance and empire, in particular the challenges of organising a monetary union, therefore shared substantial continuities which stretched from the mid-eighteenth century onwards.

Notes

1. My main references concerning imperial monetary policy and the politics and economics of colonial paper money in individual colonies are Leslie V. Brock, *The currency of the American colonies, 1700–1764: a study in colonial finance and imperial relations* (New York, 1975); Joseph Albert Ernst, *Money and politics in America, 1755–1775: a study in the Currency Act of 1764 and the political economy of revolution* (Chapel Hill, NC, 1973). Articles by Jack M. Sosin, 'Imperial regulation of colonial paper money, 1764–1773', *Pennsylvania Magazine of History and Biography*, 87 (1964); Roger W. Weiss, 'The issue of paper money in the American colonies,

1720–1774', *Journal of Economic History*, 30 (1970); Jack P. Greene and Richard M. Jellison, 'The Currency Act of 1764 in imperial-colonial relations, 1764–1776', *William and Mary Quarterly*, 18 (1961) are essentially overviews of the topic, while Alvin Rabushka, *Taxation in colonial America* (Princeton, 2008) focuses on the fiscal rather than monetary aspects of paper money. John J. McCusker, *Money and exchange in Europe and America, 1600–1775: a handbook* (London, 1978) is a crucial work of reference. Other works dealing with particular aspects of imperial and colonial paper money are cited as they arise.
2. For an overview, see McCusker, *Money and exchange* pp. 116–31; John J. McCusker and Russell R. Menard, *The economy of British America, 1607–1789* (Chapel Hill, NC, 1991) pp. 335–41.
3. For the use of this term, see Daniel Carey and Christopher Finlay (eds.), *The empire of credit: the financial revolution in the British Atlantic world, 1688–1815* (Dublin, 2011).
4. Jonathan Edward Barth, '"A peculiar stampe of our owne": the Massachusetts Mint and the battle over sovereignty, 1652–1691', *New England Quarterly*, 87 (2014) pp. 490–525; Curtis P. Nettels, *The money supply of the American colonies before 1720* (Madison, WI, 1934) pp. 170–8.
5. See below on proclamation money, n. 53.
6. Katherine Smoak, 'The weight of necessity: counterfeit coins in the British Atlantic world, circa 1760–1800', *William and Mary Quarterly*, 74 (2017) pp. 467–502.
7. Brock, *Currency* pp. 9–16, 99–106; Nettels, *Money supply* pp. 179–85, 202–27, 525–6; Ernst, *Money and politics* pp. 18–23, 139–53. These resembled to some degree the 'lumbard banks' proposed in Britain in the late seventeenth century: John Keith Horsefield, *British monetary experiments, 1650–1710* (London, 1960) pp. 104–13.
8. E. James Ferguson, 'Currency finance: an interpretation of colonial monetary practices', *William and Mary Quarterly*, 10 (1953) pp. 153–80 and Chap. 3.
9. See Chap. 2.
10. See Chap. 3.
11. McCusker and Menard, *Economy of British America* pp. 20–31, 71–88; Allan Kulikoff, *From British peasants to colonial American farmers* (Chapel Hill, NC and London, 2000) pp. 216–26.
12. S. D. Smith, 'Merchants and planters revisited', *Economic History Review*, 55 (2002) pp. 434–65; Richard B. Sheridan, *Sugar and slavery: an economic history of the British West Indies, 1623–1775* (Barbados, 1974) pp. 262–305; Jacob M. Price, *Capital and credit in British overseas trade: the view from the Chesapeake, 1700–1776* (Cambridge, MA, 1980), esp. pp. 96–123; Ernst, *Money and politics* pp. 43–51; James H. Soltow,

'Scottish traders in Virginia, 1750–1775', *Economic History Review*, 12 (1959) pp. 83–98; T. M. Devine, *The tobacco lords: a study of the tobacco merchants of Glasgow and their trading activities, c. 1740–90* (Edinburgh, 1990) pp. 82–98.

13. Ernst, *Money and politics* pp. 70–7, 308–11; Richard B. Sheridan, 'The British credit crisis of 1772 and the American colonies', *Journal of Economic History*, 20 (1960) pp. 161–86; S. G. Checkland, *Scottish banking: a history, 1695–1973* (Glasgow, 1975) pp. 118–24; Tyler Beck Goodspeed, *Legislating instability: Adam Smith, free banking, and the financial crisis of 1772* (Cambridge, MA, 2016) pp. 10–21, 31–46; Paul Kosmetatos, *The 1772–73 British credit crisis* (London, 2018) pp. 41–122.

14. For local sources of capital and credit (often in the form of book credit) across the British Atlantic, see Julian Gwyn, *The enterprising admiral: the personal fortune of Admiral Sir Peter Warren* (Montreal, 1974) pp. 95–118; Jessica C. Roney, *Governed by a spirit of opposition: the origins of American political practice in colonial Philadelphia* (Baltimore, MD, 2014) pp. 105–30; Robert E. Wright, *Origins of commercial banking in America, 1750–1800* (Lanham, MD, 2001) pp. 19–33; Kulikoff, *From British peasants* pp. 216–26; S. D. Smith, *Slavery, family, and gentry capitalism in the British Atlantic: the world of the Lascelles, 1648–1834* (Cambridge; New York, 2006) pp. 131–77; Simon Middleton, 'Private credit in eighteenth-century New York City: the Mayor's Court Papers, 1681–1776', *Journal of Early American History*, 2 (2012) pp. 150–77; Wilbur C. Plummer, 'Consumer credit in Philadelphia', *The Pennsylvania Magazine of History and Biography*, 66 (1942) pp. 385–409; Mary M. Schweitzer, *Custom and contract: household, government, and the economy in colonial Pennsylvania* (New York and Guildford, 1987) pp. 142–7.

15. McCusker, *Money and exchange* pp. 157–9, 175–7; Nettels, *Money supply* pp. 229–49; Ronald Michener, 'Fixed exchange rates and the quantity theory in colonial America', *Carnegie-Rochester Conference Series on Public Policy*, 27 (1987) pp. 253–76.

16. Ernst, *Money and politics* pp. 34–9; Margaret Ellen Newell, *From dependency to independence: economic revolution in colonial New England* (Ithaca, NY and London, 1998) pp. 183–7, 228–35; Brock, *Currency* pp. 35–49, 185–242, 409–11, 524, 559–60; Edwin J. Perkins, 'Conflicting views on fiat currency: Britain and its North American colonies in the eighteenth century', *Business History*, 33 (1991) pp. 20–1; Greene and Jellison, 'Currency Act', pp. 485–6. By contrast, before 1740 the Board's attitude to paper money was 'reluctantly sympathetic and essentially reasonable': Brock, *Currency* pp. 172–85, 237–42, 558, quotation on p. 184.

17. E. James Ferguson, *The power of the purse: a history of American public finance, 1776–1790* (Chapel Hill, 1961) pp. 3–24; Ernst, *Money and poli-*

tics, esp. pp. 3–17; Robert Craig West, 'Money in the colonial American economy', *Economic Inquiry*, 16 (1978) pp. 1–15; Elmus Wicker, 'Colonial monetary standards contrasted: evidence from the Seven Years War', *Journal of Economic History*, xlv (1985); Bruce D. Smith, 'American colonial monetary regimes: the failure of the quantity theory and some evidence in favour of an alternate view', *Canadian Journal of Economics / Revue canadienne d'Economique*, 18 (1985) pp. 531–65; Farley Grubb, 'Is paper money just paper money? Experimentation and variation in the paper monies issued by the American colonies from 1690 to 1775', *Research in Economic History*, 32 (2016) pp. 147–224.
18. See also Jacob M. Price, 'The money question', *Reviews in American History*, 2 (1974) pp. 364–73; Brock, *Currency*, esp. pp. 17–21, 528–57 and the unpaginated 'Preface'; Michener, 'Fixed exchange rates', pp. 277–95; Bennett T. McCallum, 'Money and prices in colonial America: a new test of competing theories', *Journal of Political Economy*, 100 (1992) pp. 143–61; Scott Sumner, 'Colonial currency and the quantity theory of money: a critique of Smith's interpretation', *Journal of Economic History*, 53 (1993) pp. 139–45.
19. For the most recent restatements of this approach, see Ronald Michener and Robert E. Wright, 'Development of the US monetary union', *Financial History Review*, 13 (2006) pp. 19–41; Ronald Michener, 'Redemption theories and the value of American colonial paper money', *Financial History Review*, 22 (2016) pp. 315–35.
20. For specific contemporary authors, see Richard A. Lester, 'Currency issues to overcome depressions in Pennsylvania, 1723 and 1729', *Journal of Political Economy*, 46 (1938) pp. 324–75; Perkins, 'Conflicting views', pp. 12–17; Newell, *Dependency to independence* pp. 138–80, 203–7, 218–25; Elizabeth E. Dunn, '"Grasping at the shadow": the Massachusetts currency debate, 1690–1751', *New England Quarterly*, 71 (1998) pp. 54–76; Katie A. Moore, 'America's first economic stimulus package: paper money and the body politic in colonial Pennsylvania, 1715–1730', *Pennsylvania History*, 83 (2016) pp. 529–57; Jeffrey Sklansky, *Sovereign of the market: The money question in early America* (Chicago, 2017) pp. 21–91.
21. For British views in this mid-eighteenth-century period, see Lloyd W. Mints, *A history of banking theory in Great Britain and the United States* (Chicago, 1945) pp. 13–41; L. S. Pressnell, *Country banking in the industrial revolution* (Oxford, 1956) pp. 193–224; Horsefield, *Monetary experiments* pp. 23–36, 221–47; Douglas Vickers, *Studies in the Theory of Money, 1690–1776* (London, 1960), esp. pp. 293–305; Perkins, 'Conflicting views', pp. 8–12; Christine Desan, *Making money: coin, currency, and the coming of capitalism* (2014) pp. 404–21.

22. Greene and Jellison, 'Currency Act', pp. 485–8; Sosin, 'Imperial regulation', pp. 174–78; Ernst, *Money and politics* pp. 43–88; Brock, *Currency* pp. 428–45, 477–527, 559–63; Thomas C. Barrow, *Trade and empire: the British customs service in colonial America 1660–1775* (Cambridge, MA, 1967) p. 314n; Ferguson, *Power* pp. 15–20; Perkins, 'Conflicting views', pp. 21–3. For the Currency Act of 1751, see above.
23. See Chap. 4.
24. C.W. Munn, *The Scottish provincial banking companies 1747–1864* (Edinburgh, 1981) pp. 16–21; Checkland, *Scottish banking* pp. 118–21, 253–5, 263–70; Goodspeed, *Legislating instability* pp. 28–91; Kosmetatos, *British credit crisis* pp. 104–15. Goodspeed shows that the bill was proposed by Scottish banking interests to drive their smaller competition out of the market, but it received political support because it was cast in line with accepted economic ideas. The commonalities between the colonial and Scottish currency acts of 1764 and 1765 have so far been almost entirely overlooked by their respective historiographies, despite the fact that in the 1760s and 1770s Scotland found itself in much the same economic position as the colonies, that is, desperate for capital for economic development but facing a continual drain of money to London due to an imbalance of trade (for which see H. Hamilton, 'Scotland's balance of payments problem in 1762', *Economic History Review*, 5 (1953) pp. 344–57). It should therefore be no surprise therefore that they resorted to the same financial expedients, and faced the same backlash from conservative financial interests in England.
25. Charles F. Mullett, 'English imperial thinking, 1764–1783', *Political Science Quarterly*, 45 (1930) pp. 548–79; Jack P. Greene, 'Martin Bladen's blueprint for a colonial union', *William and Mary Quarterly*, 17 (1960) pp. 516–30; J.M. Bumsted, '"Things in the womb of time": ideas of American Independence, 1633 to 1763', *William and Mary Quarterly*, 31 (1974) pp. 533–64; P. J. Marshall, 'Empire and authority in the later eighteenth century', *Journal of Imperial and Commonwealth History*, 15 (1987) pp. 105–22; David Armitage, *The ideological origins of the British Empire* (Cambridge, 2000); Craig Yirush, *Settlers, liberty, and empire: the roots of early American political theory, 1675–1775* (Cambridge, 2011) pp. 183–214.
26. Timothy J. Shannon, *Indians and colonists at the crossroads of empire: The Albany Congress of 1754* (Ithaca, NY, 2000) pp. 83–113; Carla Mulford, *Benjamin Franklin and the Ends of Empire* (2015) pp. 127–40; Alan Rogers, *Empire and liberty: American resistance to British authority, 1755–1763* (Berkeley, 1974) pp. 10–21.
27. S. Max Edelson, *The new map of empire: how Britain imagined America before independence* (Cambridge, MA, 2017) pp. 2, 38–61. For overviews,

see also Patrick Griffin and Oxford University Press., *The Townshend moment: the making of empire and revolution in the eighteenth century* (New Haven, CT, 2018) pp. 132–9; P. J. Marshall, *The making and unmaking of empires: Britain, India, and America c.1750–1783* (Oxford, 2005) pp. 161–206.
28. Edelson, *New map* pp. 141–95; Rogers, *Empire and liberty* pp. 22–36; Richard White, *The middle ground: Indians, empires, and republics in the Great Lakes region, 1650–1815* (Cambridge, 2011) pp. 269–364; Daniel K. Richter, 'Native Americans, the Plan of 1764 and a British Empire that never was', in Alan Tully and Robert Olwell (eds.), *Cultures and identities in colonial British America* (Baltimore, MD, 2005) pp. 269–92.
29. John L. Bullion, '"The ten thousand in America": more light on the decision on the American army, 1762–1763', *William and Mary Quarterly*, 43 (1986) pp. 646–57; John W. Shy, *Toward Lexington: the role of the British Army in the coming of the American Revolution* (Princeton, NJ, 1965) pp. 140–231; Edelson, *New map* pp. 85–98.
30. Neil R. Stout, *The Royal Navy in America, 1760–1775: a study of enforcement of British colonial policy in the era of the American Revolution* (Annapolis, MD, 1973), esp. pp. 25–55; Sarah Kinkel, *Disciplining the empire: politics, governance, and the rise of the British navy* (Cambridge, MA, 2018) pp. 155–80; Rabushka, *Taxation* p. 736.
31. Rabushka, *Taxation* pp. 741–7, 751–8; Edelson, *New map* pp. 293–8; Griffin, *Townshend moment* pp. 121–32; Andrew O'Shaughnessy, *An empire divided: the American Revolution and the British Caribbean* (Philadelphia, 2000) pp. 81–108; John L. Bullion, *A great and necessary measure: George Granville and the genesis of the Stamp Act 1763–1765* (Columbia, MO, 1982), esp. pp. 99–113.
32. Barrow, *Trade and empire* pp. 176–88, 208–26; Gautham Rao, *National duties: custom houses and the making of the American state* (Chicago, IL, 2016) pp. 19–47; Dora Mae Clark, 'The American Board of Customs, 1767–1783', *American Historical Review*, 45 (1940) pp. 777–806; Alfred S. Martin, 'The King's Customs: Philadelphia, 1763–1774', *William and Mary Quarterly*, 5 (1948) pp. 201–16; John J. McCusker, 'Colonial civil servant and counter-revolutionary: Thomas Irving (1738?–1800) in Boston, Charleston and London', in John J. McCusker (ed.), *Essays in the economic history of the Atlantic world* (London, 1997) pp. 190–221; Carl Ubbelohde, *The Vice-Admiralty Courts and the American Revolution* (Chapel Hill, 1960), esp. pp. 99–127; Rabushka, *Taxation* pp. 738–41; Griffin, *Townshend moment* pp. 130–1.
33. Peter Andreas, *Smuggler nation: how illicit trade made America* (New York, 2013) pp. 11–60; Thomas M. Truxes, *Defying empire: trading with the enemy in colonial New York* (New Haven, CT, 2008); Richard

B. Sheridan, 'The Molasses Act and the market strategy of the British sugar planters', *Journal of Economic History*, 17 (1957) pp. 62–83; Sheridan, *Sugar and slavery* pp. 66–71; Barrow, *Trade and empire* pp. 160–8; Bullion, *Great and necessary measure* pp. 62–77.
34. Edelson, *New map* pp. 22–46, 197–287, 286. For the Sugar Act, see Chap. 4.
35. Ibid. pp. 46–61, 103–39, 186–91; Eric Hinderaker, *Elusive empires: constructing colonialism in the Ohio Valley, 1673–1800* (Cambridge, 1997) pp. 134–75; Clarence Edwin Carter, *Great Britain and the Illinois country, 1763–1774* (Washington, DC, 1910) pp. 55–76, 103–45; Jack M. Sosin, *Whitehall and the wilderness: the Middle West in British colonial policy, 1760–1775* (Lincoln, NE, 1961) pp. 79–171.
36. Frances Armytage, *The free port system in the British West Indies: a study in commercial policy, 1766–1822* (London, 1953) pp. 28–51; Sheridan, *Sugar and slavery* pp. 460–1; Adrian John Pearce, *British trade with Spanish America, 1763–1808* (Liverpool, 2007) pp. 42–70.
37. Edelson, *New map* p. 61.
38. See n. 34 and 35.
39. A. B. McCullough, *Money and exchange in Canada to 1900* (Toronto, 1984) pp. 127–31, 281–5; McCusker, *Money and exchange* pp. 230–4. Since Nova Scotia rated the dollar at 5s currency, a dollar coin might therefore be worth as much as 5s 6d Halifax currency. As a result, the Treasury paid dollars to soldiers in Nova Scotia at the rate of 5s sterling per dollar: see TNA, T1/379/29, Baker to Devonshire, 12 May 1757; TNA, T1/391 f. 10r-v, Colebrooke and Nesbitt, 21 Feb. 1759.
40. James F. Shepherd and Samuel H. Williamson, 'The coastal trade of the British North American colonies, 1768–1772', *Journal of Economic History*, 32 (1972) pp. 783–810; William S. Sachs, 'Interurban correspondents and the development of a national economy before the Revolution: New York as a case study', *New York History*, 36 (1955) pp. 320–35; Joseph S. Tiedemann, 'Interconnected communities: the middle colonies on the eve of the American Revolution', *Pennsylvania History*, 71 (2009) pp. 1–41; James H. Soltow, 'The role of Williamsburg in the Virginia economy, 1750–1775', *William and Mary Quarterly*, 15 (1958) pp. 467–82.
41. McCusker found only limited evidence for regular intercolonial rates of exchange, suggesting that the volume of transactions was so low as to render them uncommon: McCusker, *Money and exchange* pp. 122–4, 134, 159–60, 169–70, 177–81, 195, 220–1. However, for the intercolonial circulation of colonial currencies and the existence of regional bill markets, see Nettels, *Money supply* pp. 99–127; Brock, *Currency* pp. 35–43, 66–74, 84–95, 253–4; Turk McCleskey and James C. Squire, 'Pennsylvania credit

in the Virginia backcountry, 1746–1755', *Pennsylvania History*, 81 (2014) pp. 207–21; Thomas L. Purvis, *Proprietors, patronage, and paper money: legislative politics in New Jersey, 1703–1776* (New Brunswick, NJ; London, 1986) pp. 149–50; Sachs, 'Interurban correspondents', pp. 327, 330–1; Soltow, 'Williamsburg', pp. 474–81; Wright, *Origins* pp. 52–60; Donald L. Kemmerer, 'The colonial loan-office system in New Jersey', *Journal of Political Economy*, 47 (1939) pp. 871–2 and Chap. 1 concerning Rhode Island.

42. Aaron Graham, 'Corruption and contractors in the North Atlantic, 1754–63', *English Historical Review*, 133 (2018) pp. 1093–1119; Stanley McCrory Pargellis, *Lord Loudoun in North America* (New Haven, CT, 1933) pp. 281–6; Dora Mae Clark, 'The British Treasury and the administration of military affairs in America, 1754–1774', *Pennsylvania History*, 2 (1935) pp. 197–204; Shy, *Toward Lexington* pp. 221–4; Nettels, *Money supply* pp. 195–201.
43. TNA, WO34/98 ff. 246r, 259r, 276r, 292r; TNA, WO34/197/2 pp. 336, 340; and Chap. 4.
44. Graham, 'Corruption and contractors', pp. 1107–9; Pargellis, *Loudoun* pp. 281–6.
45. TNA, T1/371/62, Tomlinson & Hanbury to the Treasury, 20 August 1756.
46. Graham, 'Corruption and contractors', pp. 1104–13.
47. Norman Baker, *Government and contractors: the British Treasury and war supplies, 1775–1783* (London, 1971) pp. 175–83; R. Arthur Bowler, *Logistics and the failure of the British Army in America, 1775–1783* (Princeton, NJ, 1975) pp. 155–66; Julian Gwyn, 'The impact of British military spending on the colonial money markets, 1760–1783', *Historical Papers/Communications Historiques*, (1980) pp. 77–95; McCullough, *Money and exchange in Canada* pp. 286–91.
48. See Chap. 4.
49. Ernst, *Money and politics* pp. 68–9; Beverley W. Bond, *The quit-rent system in the American colonies* (New Haven, 1919), passim, but esp. 17–18, 142–6, 245–8, 451–3; Moore, 'Stimulus package', pp. 533, 543–4; Soltow, 'Williamsburg', p. 477; Brock, *Currency* p. 486.
50. Andrew Edwards, 'Grenville's silver hammer: the problem of money in the Stamp Act Crisis', *Journal of American History*, 104 (2017) pp. 337–62. O'Shaughnessy highlights the problems this posed in the Caribbean as well: O'Shaughnessy, *An empire divided* pp. 84–5. For the market price in London, see McCusker, *Money and exchange* p. 17.
51. Edwards, 'Grenville's silver hammer', p. 361.
52. For counterfeit coins, see n. 6.

53. Robert Chalmers, *A history of currency in the British colonies* (London, 1893) pp. 4–16; Ernst 'Money' pp. 23–5; Nettels, 'Money supply', pp. 170–8; Brock, 'Currency' pp. 130–66, 239–40.
54. For imperial reform between 1680 and 1720, see in particular Ian K. Steele, *Politics of colonial policy: the Board of Trade in colonial administration 1696–1720* (Oxford, 1968); Edelson, *New map* pp. 22–34; Stephen Saunders Webb, 'William Blathwayt, Imperial Fixer: from Popish Plot to Glorious Revolution (pt. i)', *William and Mary Quarterly*, 3rd ser, 25 (1968) pp. 4–21; Stephen Saunders Webb, 'William Blathwayt, Imperial Fixer: muddling through to empire, 1689–1717 (pt. ii)', *William and Mary Quarterly, 3rd ser*, 26 (1969) pp. 373–415.
55. Ernst, *Money and politics* pp. 30–43; Brock, *Currency* pp. 237–42; Sosin, 'Imperial regulation', p. 185.
56. David Fox, 'The Anglo-Scots monetary union of 1707', *Edinburgh Law Review*, 23 (2019) pp. 360–87; Atholl L. Murray, 'The Scottish recoinage of 1707–9 and its aftermath', *British Numismatic Journal*, 72 (2003) pp. 115–34.
57. See Chap. 4.
58. Daniel Richter has likewise argued for the utility of examining the unimplemented 'Plan for the future management of Indian affairs' of 1764 as an indication of the state of imperial thought towards native peoples: Richter, 'Plan of 1764', pp. 269, 291–2.
59. Carl Wennerlind, *Casualties of credit: the English financial revolution, 1620–1720* (Cambridge, MA, 2011) pp. 44–79; Paul Slack, *The invention of improvement: information and material progress in seventeenth-century England* (Oxford, 2015) pp. 91–128; Horsefield, *Monetary experiments* pp. 93–100.
60. Wennerlind, *Casualties of credit* pp. 3, 83–95; Horsefield, *Monetary experiments* pp. 93–103, 228–36; P.G.M. Dickson, *The financial revolution in England: a study in the development of public credit, 1688–1756* (London, 1967) pp. 3–8, 15–35; Slack, *Invention of improvement* pp. 141–2, 173, 244–6.
61. Desan, *Making money* pp. 295–6, 331–9; Horsefield, *Monetary experiments* pp. 104–217; Dickson, *Financial revolution* pp. 39–57; Seiichiro Ito, 'The making of institutional credit in England, 1600 to 1688', *European Journal of the History of Economic Thought*, 18 (2011) pp. 487–519; Wennerlind, *Casualties of credit* pp. 95–121; Patrick Walsh, *The South Sea bubble and Ireland: money, banking and investment, 1690–1721* (London, 2014) pp. 19–34. For America, see Chaps. 2 and 3.
62. Walsh, *South Sea Bubble* pp. 125–62; M. Ryder, 'The Bank of Ireland, 1721: land, credit and dependency', *Historical Journal*, 25 (1982) pp. 557–82; Constantine Caffentzis, 'Why did Berkeley's bank fail? Money

and libertinism in eighteenth-century Ireland', *Eighteenth-century Ireland / Iris an dá chultúr*, 12 (1997) pp. 100–15; Patrick Hyde Kelly, 'Berkeley and the idea of a national bank', *Eighteenth-century Ireland / Iris an dá chultúr*, 25 (2010) pp. 98–117. For the Massachusetts banks, see Chaps. 2 and 3.
63. See Chap. 4.
64. See Chap. 4.

CHAPTER 2

Land Banks

Abstract A number of proposals for an imperial paper currency drew on the principles and practices of colonial land banks, which issued paper bank notes upon the security of mortgages on land. Successful examples such as the General Loan Office of Pennsylvania encouraged Benjamin Franklin and other writers to explore how they might be scaled up to provide the British Atlantic with credit and a paper currency to overcome the shortage of a common circulating medium. Each proposal adopted different elements of the system, however, in line with their broader views about the nature and location of imperial authority, the direction and trajectory of colonial development, and the purposes and aims of imperial and colonial reforms.

Keywords Land bank • Benjamin Franklin • Charles Williamos • Lachlan Macleane • Currency

Perhaps the best-known proposal to address the problems of a continental paper currency in British America in the eighteenth century came from Benjamin Franklin. It envisaged the creation of a cross-colonial 'land bank' for British North America, scaling up the model provided by provincial land banks such as the General Loan Office of Pennsylvania and their system of issuing paper notes to borrowers backed by the security of mortgages on land. Yet it was only one of several such proposals to emerge between 1764 and 1768, which took the basic model of the land bank and then attempted to steer their way between colonial desires for a looser monetary policy under local control on the one hand, and imperial wishes for a tighter policy and stable exchange rates under metropolitan control on the other. The emphasis reflected their particular interests and experiences. Franklin increasingly saw the British Empire by 1764 as a loose collection of closely affiliated territories, which would be allowed to develop their own way under the umbrella of British protection. Charles Williamos, a colonial official in the Carolinas, proposed a more active and interventionist land bank to support the planters, but under the control and guidance of colonial governors. Lauchlin Macleane, an imperial official in London, favoured a land bank that would guarantee stable remittances for British merchants from across British America, through firm imperial control and colonial dependency. Each writer isolated various elements from the metropolitan and colonial financial precedents and principles that they had before them to develop their proposals.

Land Banks

The basis of a land bank was that money was created by issuing notes wholly, or almost wholly, on the security of mortgages on land, which limited the amount that could be circulated and *in extremis* provided an asset to be sequestered if the debtor refused to repay their loan.[1] Hence, while the practice of lending money on the security of land is ancient, the innovative character of the land bank lay firstly in the fact that it was a financial institution incorporated specifically for this purpose; secondly, in the fact that it went about doing this through the creation of bank notes intended for general circulation, rather than by lending an existing circulating medium; and thirdly, that by issuing these notes it therefore helped to increase the total money supply. The land bank therefore intended to create both credit and currency out of thin air, providing the perfect solution for economies lacking either. In late seventeenth-century England, it promised to supersede the scrivener-bankers and county attorneys who specialised in brokering mortgages upon land.[2] Numerous plans for land banks therefore circulated in the early stages of the British financial revolution in the late seventeenth century, and plans for a National Land Bank were brought forward in 1695 as a competitor to the Bank of England.[3] It collapsed ignominiously, partially from political opposition and partially because supporters were forced to dilute the initial proposals by promising to raise a large part in specie in return for the support of the government, and then found themselves unable to do so. Thoroughly discredited by this debacle, the land bank was overtaken by other measures discussed in the next chapter, though land still made up the collateral of many Scottish banks and formed the collateral for their note issues, especially the doomed Ayr Bank of south-western Scotland between 1769 and 1772.[4]

In British America however the land bank found a more fertile soil. Drawing on the proposals circulated in Britain, a version was projected in 1686 until it was derailed by the political conflicts associated with the Dominion of New England.[5] Planters in Barbados attempted to organise a land bank in 1706, but in a pattern that would soon become familiar, they ran into strong opposition from merchants and interest groups in London, who persuaded the Board of Trade to close it down.[6] Barbados had strong links with South Carolina and therefore may have inspired the land bank established there in 1712, and after repeated efforts a public land bank was also set up in Massachusetts in 1714.[7] The floodgates then opened, with almost every colony in British America establishing a public land bank between 1715 and 1737 and renewing them repeatedly up to 1774. Most had a common set of features. They were created by legislative enactment, and their management was carried out by directors or trustees, who were generally authorised to issue only a fixed amount of notes.[8] Most allocated a quota to each county or district where local authorities, such as the town meetings in New England or the county boards in New York and New Jersey, solicited and assessed requests for loans with the help of their surveyor or local knowledge. Once approved, the borrower would be advanced up to half the value of their land in notes issued by the bank, which were often made legal tender for the payment of taxes and even private debts. The most ambitious venture came in 1739, when groups in Boston attempted to charter a private joint-stock land bank that would strike off £150,000 in notes.[9] Like many of the other ventures, it reflected a particular set of interests and ideologies, being intended primarily to provide cash and credit for small farmers and retailers in Massachusetts and New England who had been frozen out by the merchant oligarchy in Boston.

The land bank was therefore a widespread and relatively successful precedent for anyone in British America contemplating the problems of imperial currency by the mid-eighteenth century, despite its failures in Britain. The General Loan Office of Pennsylvania in particular fulfilled its primary remit of making credit available to middling farmers, retailers and artisans in reliable and secure paper notes, which enjoyed a wide circulation and were widely believed to have pulled the colony out of two economic depressions in 1723 and 1729.[10] The interest produced by the loans also proved a useful supplement to colonial revenues, to the extent that Pennsylvania and New Jersey were briefly able to abandon most other taxes, as some projectors before 1700 had hoped the British government might likewise be able to do.[11] The success of land banks in British America probably reflected a number of factors. Unlike in Britain, land was readily available and also relatively cheap, within the reach of even middling farmers and artisans, creating large numbers of borrowers able to provide the necessary landed securities. Most colonies maintained deed registries which enabled titles and liens upon land to be easily checked.[12] Scotland likewise possessed the registry of sasines or land titles, helping its own private banks to lend money on land, whereas in England only four registries were set up in this period, for Middlesex and the ridings of Yorkshire, despite the early projectors showing the land banks could not work without such a registry.[13] Land banks were also, legally, in a weaker position in Britain. Since their notes were never made a legal tender, British land banks could only maintain their value by promising to redeem the notes in specie on demand, which in turn required them either to retain a large and unproductive specie reserve or else to rely upon the liquidity provided by financial markets in London or Edinburgh.[14] No such financial markets existed in British America, except perhaps to some extent in New York and Philadelphia, but assemblies were happy to give land bank notes the status of legal tender, allowing them to circulate virtually indefinitely and to maintain their value, since they could always be used to pay for taxes or debts at their face value.

However, this advantage cut both ways. As projectors in Britain recognised at an early stage, an unscrupulous or irresponsible land bank might issue more notes than it had security for, either in anticipation of the economic growth which would enable them to be repaid or to meet pressing demands for currency and credit.[15] Making notes legal tender removed a crucial check on this, since notes could then be issued at will and forced onto unwilling creditors at their nominal value, causing massive inflation and, in the case of the colonies, the further devaluation of their currency relative to sterling. Most of the mid-Atlantic colonies managed their issues to avoid this.[16] In Maryland, further security was provided by using interest payments to purchase Bank of England stock, which could then be liquidated when the loans matured to redeem the notes left in circulation.[17] However, as was noted in the last chapter, Rhode Island was guilty of issuing large volumes of land bank notes in the 1730s and 1740s for its own profit, until the British imperial state was stirred into uncharacteristic action at the instigation of mercantile interests in Britain and America and passed the Currency Act of 1751.[18] Land banks in British America therefore avoided the issue of inadequate liquidity which had brought down the National Land Bank in 1696, and which would bring down the Ayr Bank in 1772, but had already seen the opposite problem of excessive liquidity. The success by 1764 of land banks in Pennsylvania, New Jersey and elsewhere in addressing this problem suggested though that they might nevertheless be suitable templates for banks aimed at circulating paper money on a continental scale.

Franklin (1754–1767)

The first person to consider using a land bank to support a continental currency and as an instrument of imperial unity was Benjamin Franklin in 1764. The proposal he put forward has been widely noted but less rarely studied, and even then merely as an aspect of his economic and imperial thought.[19] He stressed, from an early stage, the political and economic unity of the British Atlantic and the role that a properly managed paper currency could play in providing the financial and monetary means for colonial economic expansion.[20] Proposals such as the Albany Plan of Union that he offered in 1754, which envisaged a limited central government in British America with military and fiscal powers, exemplified Franklin's capacity and willingness to translate these principles into concrete projects.[21] Around the same time, Franklin had also received a proposal from Richard Jackson, a British merchant and agent for several American colonies, for 'a plan of a provincial bank'.[22] As the next chapter will show, this proposed to splice the existing Pennsylvania Loan Office or land bank in Philadelphia into a new bank whose notes would circulate not just in Pennsylvania but throughout British America.[23] Though sometimes misread as the origin of Franklin's later proposals for a continental land bank, this was in fact very different one based on monetary principles and practice in England; by contrast, the proposals that Franklin offered between 1764 and 1767 reflected his own positive experience of land banks in Pennsylvania.[24] In the same way that Franklin 'adapted and created innovations in existing economic discourse to the situation of Philadelphia' in his pamphlet *A modest enquiry into the nature and necessity of a paper currency* in 1729 to support the new Loan Office, his proposals in 1764 took those same principles, refined by over 30 years of practice, and extrapolated them into a plan for a continental currency and land bank for British America.[25]

The trigger for these proposals was Franklin's arrival in Britain in December 1764 as the envoy of leading interests in Pennsylvania, and the news that the prime minister George Grenville was already entertaining proposals for a measure to replace the new Currency Act and its total ban on all paper currencies with a measure that could command colonial support.[26] With assistance from Thomas Pownall, a politician and former governor of Massachusetts who was deeply interested in colonial monetary matters, Franklin proposed to establish a land bank upon a continental scale, and use it to provide a paper currency which would promote the colonial economy and provide profits to the British government.[27] Having summarised the workings and success of the Loan Office since 1729, 'which has by long experience been found so practicable and so useful [and] may with a few changes to accommodate it to more general purposes be safely and advantageously extended to all the colonies', they proposed to establish a loan office in each colony 'to make some provision of a currency' by issuing paper notes. As in all colonial land banks, trustees would examine applications, take the necessary securities, issue the notes and then receive back both the interest and the principal as they fell due. A fixed quantum of notes would be issued, several million pounds at least. These notes were to be made a legal tender and, to protect the currency, counterfeiting the notes would be a capital crime. They would be denominated in currency at the rate fixed by the proclamation of 1704, of 6s currency per dollar or £133 6s 8d currency per £100 sterling, and Franklin proposed to make them exchangeable at the loan offices for bills on London at this rate. Here he was copying the practice adopted by the land bank in Maryland.[28] His main influence, however, was the General Loan Office in Philadelphia, and assessing which elements Franklin copied directly and which he altered help to clarify his specific intentions for his continental land bank.

On the one hand, the General Loan Office provided the basic inspiration for much of the structure of the land bank and some of its auditing and bookkeeping practices, which diverged in key respects from the standard practices adopted in other colonial land banks. Whereas most devolved the assessment of individual applications to the local authorities at the district level, Franklin copied the practice in Pennsylvania of establishing a central loan office, though the trustees, up to eight in total, would be elected by the individual districts.[29] They would serve under much the same terms as the trustees in Pennsylvania, enjoying a salary of £100 and a tenure of five years, at the end of which they were to hand over all their papers and submit to an audit. They would meet regularly at this central office to sign bills, to examine applications and the mortgage deeds submitted with them and to oversee the other paperwork. Borrowers would submit not only the deeds but also a penal bond committing them to comply with the terms of the loan and a warrant or power of attorney allowing the trustees to sue for the recovery of both real and personal assets from borrowers in default, a measure introduced by the General Loan Office due to the difficulties experienced in recovering lands in default. Some other measures Franklin proposed, such as the keeping of a Book of Allowances, 'so called because therein is put down what sums the trustees think proper to allow or lend to each applier, according to their opinion of the security offered', as well as a day-book and ledger for making up monthly abstracts and reports, probably reflected unwritten practices developed in the General Loan Office since 1723 to facilitate its operation.[30] His plan to employ a solicitor to examine the deeds was logical, and avoided the clunky formulas included in the Pennsylvania loan office acts for valuing land.[31] A clause allowing the bank to make loans on deposits of plate was omitted, probably because it was so rarely used.

On the other hand, some of the differences between the General Loan Office and Franklin's proposal for continental loan offices were substantive and substantial. To meet British concerns about excess paper money and 'to prevent an over-quantity existing', the loan offices would encourage borrowers to deposit their surplus paper money back in the bank by paying 5 per cent interest on any notes deposited with them, '[so] the proportion will find itself and adapt itself from time to time to the occasions of commerce'. Whereas the Pennsylvania legislature had placed a firm ceiling on the amounts any individual could receive, Franklin proposed that any person with adequate security could borrow as much as they wanted, ensuring that the loan was fully used. Perhaps the most noticeable changes were those of oversight. Franklin proposed that each loan office have a 'principal acting trustee', who would reside there and receive £200 per year, offering greater control than the uniform boards of trustees in the General Loan Office. Exercising an overall supervision would be also two commissioners in Britain appointed by the Treasury, who would arrange the printing and signing of the bills, draw up instructions to the loan offices and collate their monthly abstracts and reports for the Treasury. They in turn would appoint two roving inspectors who would audit the accounts of each office annually with the governor and council of each province, rather than the annual audit by the assembly of the General Loan Office, though Franklin thought that the assemblies might also choose to retain the power to inspect the loan office, 'for their own satisfaction and information', reporting any discrepancies they found to the governor and council. The continental loan offices therefore had a higher degree of centralisation and gave a greater role to imperial officials than the General Loan Office had done.

Two further points stand out. Firstly, when Pownall published Franklin's proposal in the fourth edition of *The Administration of the Colonies* in 1768, he extended the parts of it discussing the benefits for colonists with new elements stressing the advantages for empire. Both proposals promised to supply a common legal tender paper currency that would enable specie to be sent to Britain for buying manufactures, and 'the settlement and improvement of new tracts of land would be greatly encouraged and promoted, population increased, trade extended, etc.'[32] However, while Franklin also promised merely that 'a great annual sum continually increasing will arise to the Crown for interest, to be applied to American purpose[s]', without specifying who would have the power to dictate its application, Pownall added a further clause noting that it 'may be applied to American purpose[s] in ease of this Kingdom and became a *permanent and effective revenue*'.[33] He thus laid stress upon exactly the element that later caused Franklin to disown his plan in 1767.[34] Pownall also deleted Franklin's proposal for the land bank to offer bills of exchange on London at fixed rates, possibly as an unnecessary and impractical complication, and introduced a paragraph favourably contrasting this imperial currency with 'a paper currency poured like a deluge over a country by act[s] of assembly only', such as in Rhode Island or South Carolina, which Franklin would probably have resented.[35] Pownall also probably introduced a statement that the bank would enable the imperial government to issue 'on occasion any quantity [of notes] for service in case of an American war, without needing to send *real cash thither by hurtful contracts*', speaking to the growing concerns about the costs and difficulties of remitting money to military forces in British America. He therefore tailored Franklin's original proposal to the needs and preconceptions of British ministers and merchants.

Secondly, even the final version of the proposal published in 1768 for British consumption granted substantial administrative autonomy to the colonists to manage the new paper currency as they saw fit. The Treasury and the Commissioners would all receive regular reports from both the trustees and the inspectors, but could not intervene directly, while the role of the inspectors was purely administrative, having only the power to bring discrepancies to the attention of the governor and council of a colony, who would then lay the matter before the assembly for action.[36] The management of monetary policy and the responsibility for correcting any excesses would therefore lie mainly with the assemblies, as it did at present, with the imperial government doing little more than limiting the overall amount of money for British America. This was of a piece with Franklin's earlier proposals in the Albany Plan of Union in 1754, which had similarly vested political, military and financial authority in the elected Grand Council rather than the imperial appointee, the President-General. Franklin thus suggested a continental land bank and currency that was wholly consistent with his experience and his views on economic development, colonial political autonomy and imperial authority, intended mainly to support an idealised vision of a commonwealth of autonomous colonies while offering only limited concrete concessions to British imperial authority.

WILLIAMOS (1766)

A similar proposal for a continental land bank and paper currency was set out in July 1766 to the earl of Dartmouth, the president of the Board of Trade, by Charles Williamos.[37] Williamos was a Swiss soldier who had recently arrived in South Carolina on the staff of the new governor, Lord Charles Montagu. Montagu's brother, the duke of Manchester, had already recommended Williamos to Dartmouth in the strongest possible terms in March. After a brief tour through the Carolinas, Williamos presented his plan for a continental land bank and currency to Dartmouth as one of several measures intended to revive the economy of the region through the cultivation of silk, vines and olive trees and the injection of capital and credit into the plantation economy. The colony had suffered since the 1750s from a shortage of money, which had a particularly bad effect upon an economy dependent on the labour- and capital-intensive cultivation of staples such as tobacco, rice and indigo.[38] Williamos was struck, as Franklin and Pownall had been, by 'the great distress through the whole continent for want of money … [which] will be greater each year as their paper currency drops', but his concerns were focussed more on the consequences for British manufacturers.[39] As growing numbers of British merchants were recognising, some form of paper currency was necessary to enable colonists to continue to purchase British exports, 'which can no ways be so effectually done as by making their own interest and that of Great Britain coincide in all things if possible, by taking them off from manufacturing for themselves and bringing as far as practicable the nature of their estates to depend on Great Britain', thereby sealing their political subordination with economic dependency.

Williamos therefore looked at the issue of the continental paper currency from an imperial rather than a colonial perspective, and moulded a familiar financial practice into a form intended to strengthen the imperial connexion. To this end he proposed the foundation of 'a general bank for America … by the Government at home, with notes of different value in sterling and other currency', which would be lent to landowners on mortgaging their lands. The colonial assemblies would make regular estimates of the value of these lands, which would determine the number of notes emitted each year by the bank's Court of Directors in New York. A distributor in each colony would then issue the notes to borrowers, at 3 per cent interest, on the security of certificates issued by the colonial receiver-general and surveyor-general of quit-rents confirming the real value of their lands. As with Franklin's proposal, the amount of notes issued would therefore be determined by the value of the lands on which they were issued, allowing indefinite expansion as the frontier retreated and settlement advanced. The notes themselves would be current 'through the whole Continent and even at home', and there would be no requirement to redeem them in specie. Instead, they could be received in payment of the interest and principal on the loans and then issued out again as necessary, supported by imperial legislation making them legal tender 'for payment of all debts whatsoever', both private and public, though this conflicted with Williamos' covering letter to Dartmouth, which proposed that the scheme would be wildly popular with people, 'as it would be entirely at their own option to take the notes or not'.[40] Since the notes would be in denominations of £10 or higher, which were inconvenient for daily use, he also proposed to import a small amount of silver coin as small change and either lower its intrinsic value or raise its face value by a quarter to prevent it being exported and taken out of circulation.

Williamos therefore used the same basic concept of the colonial land bank adopted by Franklin for the smallholders of Pennsylvania, but he adapted it to the needs of South Carolina and the other plantation colonies he had toured in 1766. He argued, for example, that his plan would enable every man 'without difficulty [to] get cash to improve their estates, which now lay [sic] mostly useless, as *all the planters in general* cannot even procure enough to bring up and subsist their families and much less make upon their lands the improvement they could wish'.[41] Improvement would benefit British manufacturers by increasing the market for exports, bought either with coin or with this new paper money. Strikingly, Williamos also proposed to issue at least £10 million in notes compared to the £1 million or £2 million Franklin had envisaged, tripling the money supply in North America overnight but leaving it firmly under imperial control. This would help generate loyalty by making easy credit available for planters, but the 3 per cent interest on loans would also produce £300,000 per year in profits for the imperial government. This far outstripped the £60,000 or so that could be expected from Franklin's proposal, and would create a permanent revenue to be used 'towards the maintaining of the troops or other necessary expenses of the Government' at a time of growing fiscal pressure.

Finally, whereas Franklin had proposed a decentralised network of local loan offices under colonial management, consistent with his view of colonial political authority, Williamos proposed instead to create a Court of Directors who would meet annually in New York and exert their power directly. Borrowers in each province who held £100 or more in notes would annually elect a provincial member, but the Court would also include, *ex officio*, the governor of New York, the commander-in-chief, 'or other great officers that the Lords of the Treasury should appoint ought [sic] to be members'. The 15 directors and distributors—presumably Williamos hoped to extend the land bank to Canada, Nova Scotia or the Floridas—would each receive £1000 a year, with £3000 for a receiver-general and his staff, but would therefore share authority with other imperial officials in British North America, diluting their influence and strengthening imperial authority. The directors elected for each of the provinces would also have a seat *ex officio* in their respective colonial councils, helping to guarantee the presence of partisans politically and economically dependent upon British patronage. The Treasury in Britain would 'have the supreme direction of the bank', not only auditing its accounts, as Franklin had proposed, but also setting the quotas of notes and coins for each province and appointing the distributors who would handle all regular business. The responsibilities of the Court of Directors would be restricted to taking securities from the provincial distributors, receiving and examining all of their monthly returns, and making up the yearly returns for the Treasury, who would have had the final say in the operation of the institution.

Both Franklin and Williamos therefore looked to the colonial land banks as models for creating a uniform system of imperial currency and credit, and even agreed upon the benefits this offered for colonial economic development, but in other respects they diverged wildly. For Williamos, the chief point of creating 'a general bank in the continent, with smaller ones depending from it in each of the colonies, to distribute notes of different value which should be current through the whole continent', was to secure that continent for Britain by reinforcing its economic dependency upon the Mother Country.[42] He had noted with concern on his trip around South Carolina, for instance, that larger numbers of families in the region were producing hemp, flax and cotton which they were weaving themselves for cloth, due to the lack of money for purchasing British manufactures, 'and [that] they think it will be the means of keeping them free and independent'.[43] The money raised by the land bank he had proposed would be used to encourage the cultivation of silk, vines and olive trees which, in orthodox mercantilist fashion, would prevent Britain importing them from foreign countries. 'We are obliged to take those commodities from foreigners, who take very few of ours in return', he noted, 'and could we be supplied by any means in those articles from our own colonies nothing certainly could make either the Mother Country or its provinces abroad flourish more'. Whereas Franklin hoped to use the land bank to make British America into a larger version of Pennsylvania, prosperous and autonomous, Williamos evidently hoped to use his proposal to make it into a larger version of South Carolina, far more productive but also far more dependent.

Macleane (1765)

This balance between colonial and imperial interests in the construction of a land bank and continental currency was tilted even further towards Britain in a third proposal, submitted in 1765 by Lauchlin Macleane to the earl of Hertford, then Lord Lieutenant of Ireland. Hertford passed it on to the earl of Shelburne, another Anglo-Irish politician with an interest in imperial reform, when Shelburne became secretary of state for the southern department in 1766.[44] Macleane was appointed Shelburne's under-secretary in October 1766 with particular responsibility for North America and the West Indies, possibly on the strength of this proposal.[45] Unlike many of the other projectors, Macleane brought to the proposal not only a practical experience of colonial government but also a genuinely imperial view that encompassed Canada and the West Indies as well as the Thirteen Colonies. As a result, his proposal envisioned a far wider role for the imperial government and a correspondingly reduced role for colonial interests, and sought to provide a clear framework for the extremes of colonial experience. To address the issues arising from the misuse of colonial bills of credit and to promote development, loan offices would be created in each colony and given fixed quotas of an imperial loan, which would be denominated in their respective currencies but pegged to the silver dollar. The result would be a combination of an imperial land bank and an exchange rate mechanism, providing money to enable creditors to pay off their debts while also facilitating trade by making intercolonial exchanges simple and predictable.

Macleane was born into a Scotch-Irish family in Ulster and was 'highly intelligent, resourceful, brave, wholly without scruple, disreputable in his private as well as his public life, but capable of winning the (mistaken) confidence of a wide variety of people', according to Lucy Sutherland, '… [and] the most spectacular of the Irish and Scottish adventurers of his day … his life was a series of picaresque incidents'.[46] He travelled to Pennsylvania as a surgeon in 1756 and joined the military expeditions to Montreal in 1759 and Martinique in 1761 before diversifying into the speculation of colonial lands, which took him to Paris. He was closely connected with the more radical British politicians such as John Wilkes, Edmund Burke and Isaac Barré, which enabled him to return from Paris to be appointed lieutenant-governor of the Ceded Island of St Vincent in March 1766. In October he was brought into government by Shelburne, but also continued to deal in East India Company stock for himself and others, including the financier and speculator Sir George Colebrooke, in order to take advantage of the investment boom which followed the end of the war.[47] Between 1766 and 1769 he also acted as Shelburne's point of contact with the East India Company itself, working with major figures such as Laurence Sullivan to manage, or manipulate, its complex internal politics.[48] Macleane was therefore the epitome of the imperial adventurer, but one with an experience of empire that covered the entire British

Atlantic, as well as a sense of practical politics and a familiarity with financial and commercial markets in Britain. His letter to Hertford in 1765 included notes critiquing the policies for settling the Ceded Islands and reforming customs collection, thus addressing the means of imperial reform as well as its ends.

The proposal itself came as an incidental addendum to a longer discussion of the financial and monetary problems facing British America, which was predictably orthodox in its diagnosis, at least from the imperial point of view. The high wartime spending had encouraged Americans to invest heavily in British manufactures, and the contraction of credit after 1763 had caused an outflow of specie to settle these debts which had temporarily left the region without sufficient cash. Measures had to be taken to ease this situation until colonists were able to repay their debts, not least by abolishing the taxes levied by earlier ministries. 'The first years of a Peace would seem a very improper time to introduce violent innovations, to lay on new taxes and to abolish paper credit', he concluded, and could not fail 'to increase the confusion, to raise a spirit of clamours and discontent, and to occasion an opposition to measures which otherwise would have been thought highly reasonable'. Like others in the Rockingham ministry, which withdrew the Stamp Act but insisted upon the passage of the Declaratory Act of 1766 confirming Parliament's right to legislate for and impose taxes upon the American colonies, Macleane therefore supported the principle of colonial taxation and only disagreed with the timing. It was but fair, he thought, that Americans should contribute towards lightening a financial burden contracted, at least in part, for the support of those colonies. 'The *time* therefore, and perhaps the *mode*, of imposing the tax in question are the only circumstances which can admit of complaint', he argued, 'while the tax itself is not only equitable but necessary'. Both factors reinforced the need for stable colonial currencies, to enable the Americans to pay the taxes once they were eventually imposed.

However, Macleane felt that the existing colonial currencies were not fit for this purpose. The main fault lay with the American colonies themselves. Some had been responsible and restrained, to the extent that the Maryland bills carried a premium, but 'great abuses' had been practised in New England before 1751 by issuing bills without any means of backing them, lead to tenfold devaluation. Macleane therefore struck a moderate position, concurring with supporters in both Britain and America that bills of credit, whether issued by land banks or the colonial assemblies, were not just useful but necessary for enabling the colonists to revive commerce and make remittances home for the benefit of British merchants. What was essential however was that the paper money was adequately backed, by taxes or land, to prevent it depreciating in value as the public lost confidence that it would be redeemed.[49] 'The error did not lie in issuing bills of credit, but in not providing adequate funds for sinking the same', he wrote, and if this error could be corrected there would be no need for such damaging checks on colonial initiative. 'Nay, on the contrary', he noted, '…in a country much in debt and daily wanting for cash for remittance, there is an absolute necessity for such a quantity of paper credit as will serve as a medium for commerce', allowing the gold and silver coin to be exported to pay for the British manufactures it imported. His focus was therefore primarily upon how to prevent further depreciation of colonial currencies and protect both the British manufacturer and merchant, on the one hand, and the British state, on the other, from the irresponsible management of their paper currencies.

To square this circle, Macleane proposed to create loan offices in each colony by an act of Parliament, which would each be allocated part of a £2 million sterling loan made by the British government, to be lent out 'upon the credit of their lands' at an interest of 6 per cent per annum. From this total, some £150,000 was provisionally earmarked for Canada and Nova Scotia, and £410,000 for the Caribbean, with the remainder intended for the continental colonies, including the Floridas. Within this there was a clear hierarchy, with the first-rank colonies of Massachusetts, New York, Pennsylvania, Virginia, South Carolina and Jamaica receiving £150,000 each and the second-rank colonies of Canada, Maryland and Barbados getting £100,000, leaving the smaller ones between £20,000 and £70,000 each. He therefore envisaged a land bank system covering the entirety of British Atlantic. To prevent the inevitable imbalances of trade, 'all the bills being collected to the provinces of most extensive trade, which in some measure would defeat the intention', the provinces would issue their quota of the loan in notes denominated in their respective colonial currencies, with the rate of exchange between them 'regulated by the intrinsic value of the Spanish milled dollar, which is the prevailing coin of the colonies', as it was in practice. His bank was therefore the antithesis of the others, proposing not so much a single paper currency and colonial monetary union but a single imperial monetary framework or exchange rate mechanism which would stabilise the existing system of colonial paper currencies by placing it firmly under British imperial control.

This was, as Macleane pointed out, 'only taking into the hands of Government that power which the provinces have ever been too apt to abuse', and a better means of imperial control than the blanket ban imposed by the Currency Act of 1764. The stronger imperial control was carried over into the arrangements for its management. Franklin had given control to colonial interests, and Williamos to colonial officials, but Macleane proposed to place each loan office under a cashier, with two clerks to handle paperwork, an appraiser to value the land and a solicitor for drawing up the necessary deeds. Cashiers would remit the profits to one of the three receivers-general, and would if necessary have the discretionary power to issue notes over and above their provincial quotas 'to keep the entire loan in circulation' in case there was not sufficient business in other provinces. This was however the furthest limits of their discretion, since the quotas would be dictated by the imperial government, leaving local officials to carry on the mundane business of checking loans, receiving payments and pursuing defaulters. Since all the principal officers were to give bonds as security for their conduct, these would further enable the imperial government to check misbehaviour. Macleane predicted that the loans of paper money would produce about £120,000 per year, covering the costs of management and leaving at least £80,000 for imperial administration. '[Such] a measure, which is at the same time calculated for the advantage of individuals and for the service of the state, cannot well fail of being popular', he concluded, and the most pressing issue he thought the British state would face would be 'whether it would be for the interest of the Mother Country that her Colonies were much less indebted to her'.

Conclusion

Several proposals for an imperial paper currency between 1764 and 1768 agreed that land could and should back the new currency. This reflected the success of the land bank in British America both as a source of credit and as collateral for paper notes. Franklin's bank though was intended mainly to serve the interests of small farmers in Pennsylvania, whereas the proposal offered by Williamos would have released even more money for the use of the planters in South Carolina and the new colonial territories in North America, while Macleane intended mainly to serve the interests of British merchants seeking a stable exchange rate for remitting their profits home from across the British Atlantic. By the same token, although all three envisaged a certain level of imperial control, this varied in almost direct proportion to their respective views of empire. Franklin did not envisage the imperial government exercising anything more than a benevolent paternalistic oversight of American development, consistent with his wider view of the relationship between Britain and its imperial territories. As an imperial official who would soon work in the heart of Whitehall, Macleane naturally favoured direct imperial rule from Britain, while Williamos split the difference and proposed to vest authority in local imperial officials, befitting his position on the staff of a colonial governor. Each man therefore conceived of their continental currency and land bank as an adjunct to their wider views on empire. They were not, however, the only ones to be contemplating the topic; others were also interested, and drew on a different set of precedents and principles, as the next chapter will show.

NOTES

1. For an overview of the principles and functions of colonial land banks, see Theodore Thayer, 'The Land-Bank system in the American colonies', *Journal of Economic History*, 13 (1953) pp. 145–59.
2. Frank T. Melton, *Sir Robert Clayton and the origins of English deposit banking, 1658–1685* (Cambridge, 1986) pp. 32–9, 68–94, 111–13; Pressnell, *Country banking* pp. 36–44, 137–9, 265; Robert Robson, *The attorney in eighteenth-century England* (Cambridge, 1959) pp. 104–18.
3. Horsefield, *Monetary experiments* pp. 156–217; Dickson, *Financial revolution* pp. 6, 25; Dennis Rubini, 'Politics and the battle for the banks, 1688–1697', *English Historical Review*, 85 (1970) pp. 693–714; Richard Kleer, '"Fictitious Cash": English public finances and paper money, 1689–1697', in Charles Mcgrath and Christopher Fauske (eds.), *Money, power and print: interdisciplinary studies on the financial revolution in the British Isles* (Newark, DE, 2008) pp. 70–102; Richard Kleer, *Money, politics and power: banking and public finance in wartime England, 1694–1696* (London, 2017) pp. 95–108, 135–52, 161–4, 171–81; Desan, *Making money* pp. 367–70.
4. For the Ayr Bank, see Chap. 3.
5. Nettels, *Money supply* pp. 252–6; John Keith Horsefield, 'The origins of Blackwell's *Model* of a bank', *William and Mary Quarterly*, 23 (1966) pp. 121–35; Newell, *Dependency to independence* pp. 121–6; Katie A. Moore, 'The blood that nourishes the body politic: the origins of paper money in early America', *Early American Studies*, 17 (2019) pp. 1–23. For the Dominion, see Chap. 1.
6. Nettels, *Money supply* pp. 269–71; Ernst, *Money and politics* pp. 25–30; Brock, *Currency* pp. 142–4, 168–72.

7. Nettels, *Money supply* pp. 135–8; Thayer, 'Land-Bank system', pp. 145–8. British merchants also proposed a land bank for New England in 1715: Nettels, *Money supply* pp. 158–9; Brock, *Currency* pp. 172–3.
8. Thayer, 'Land-Bank system', pp. 148–55; Kemmerer, 'Loan-office system', pp. 867–74; Schweitzer, *Custom and contract* pp. 125–30.
9. This simplifies a complex historiography, for which see John L. Brooke, *The heart of the Commonwealth: society and political culture in Worcester County, Massachusetts, 1713–1861* (Cambridge, 1989) pp. 57–64; Rosalind Remer, 'Old Lights and New Money: a note on religion, economics and the social order in 1740 Boston', *William and Mary Quarterly*, 47 (1990) pp. 466–73; Brock, *Currency* pp. 53–6; Newell, *Dependency to independence* pp. 214–35; George Athan Billias, *The Massachusetts land bankers of 1740* ([Orono], 1959).
10. Schweitzer, *Custom and contract* pp. 131–9, 147–67; Thayer, 'Land-Bank system', pp. 151–5; Kulikoff, *From British peasants* p. 219; Lester, 'Currency issues', pp. 324–75; Moore, 'Stimulus package', pp. 529–57; Brock, *Currency* pp. 74–95.
11. Thayer, 'Land-Bank system', pp. 156–7; Rabushka, *Taxation* pp. 443, 495–8, 508–11, 517–18, 609, 628, 638, 646.
12. See, for example, Donna Bingham Munger, *Pennsylvania land records: a history and guide for research* (Wilmington, DE, 1991), passim. For the high rates of land ownership, see Kulikoff, *From British peasants* pp. 112–34, 150, 159–61. Katie Moore notes that land banks failed in British America before 1690 while land titles remained uncertain: Moore, 'Blood that nourishes', pp. 1–23; Dror Goldberg, 'Why was America's first bank aborted?', *Journal of Economic History*, 71 (2011) pp. 211–21.
13. Melton, *Sir Robert Clayton* pp. 126–78; Horsefield, *Monetary experiments* pp. 98–9, 107, 149, 210; Julian Hoppit, 'The landed interest and the national interest, 1660–1800', in Julian Hoppit (ed.), *Parliaments, nations and identities in Britain and Ireland, 1660–1850* (Manchester, 2003) pp. 91–3; Checkland, *Scottish banking* p. 192.
14. See Chap. 3 on Ayr Bank and Horsefield, *Monetary experiments* pp. 158–64, 174–8.
15. Melton, *Sir Robert Clayton* pp. 122–5; Horsefield, *Monetary experiments* pp. 156–217.
16. See Chap. 1, n. 17.
17. Thayer, 'Land-Bank system', pp. 153–5; Brock, *Currency* pp. 100–6; Ernst, *Money and politics* pp. 139–53; Sosin, 'Imperial regulation', p. 188.
18. See Chap. 1.
19. Greene and Jellison, 'Currency Act', p. 492; Ferguson, *Power* pp. 23–4; Sosin, 'Imperial regulation', p. 187; Ernst, *Money and politics* pp. 97–9; Thayer, 'Land-Bank system', p. 158.

20. For Franklin's economic and imperial thought, see Mulford, *Benjamin Franklin* pp. 75–86; Alan Craig Houston, *Benjamin Franklin and the politics of improvement* (New Haven and London, 2008) pp. 22–59; Allan Kulikoff, 'Benjamin Franklin and the theater of empire', *Pennsylvania Magazine of History and Biography*, 141 (2017) pp. 77–90.
21. See n. 20.
22. Carl Van Doren, *Letters and papers of Benjamin Franklin and Richard Jackson, 1753–1785* (Philadelphia, PA, 1947) pp. 42–54.
23. See Chap. 3.
24. For these misreadings, see Ferguson, *Power* p. 23; Ernst, *Money and politics* pp. 96–100; Sosin, 'Imperial regulation', p. 187; Lawrence Gipson, *The British Empire before the American Revolution* (15 vols., Caldwell, ID and New York, 1936–1970) vol. xi, 261.
25. Mulford, *Benjamin Franklin* p. 78. For the operation of the General Loan Office, see n. 10.
26. Ernst, *Money and politics* pp. 96–100; Sosin, 'Imperial regulation', p. 187.
27. *The Papers of Benjamin Franklin* ed. Leonard W. Labaree et al. (43 vols, New Haven, CT and London, 1959-) vol. xii, 47–60, 'Scheme for supplying the colonies with a paper currency' (circa 11–12 February 1765) and Thomas Pownall, *The administration of the colonies: wherein their rights and constitution are discussed and stated* (1768) pp. 243–53. For Pownall, see John A. Schutz, *Thomas Pownall: British defender of American liberty. A study of Anglo-American relations in the Eighteenth century* (Glendale, CA, 1951); G.H. Guttridge, 'Thomas Pownall's *The Administration of the Colonies*: the six editions', *William and Mary Quarterly*, 26 (1969) pp. 31–46.
28. See n. 17.
29. This is based on the official acts in *Statutes at Large of Pennsylvania from 1682–1801* ed. James T. Mitchell and Henry Flanders (14 vols, Harrisburg, PA, 1896–1909) vol. iii, 324–38, 360–2, 385–407, 427–43 and n. 10 above.
30. For bookkeeping in English scrivener-banks, see Melton, *Sir Robert Clayton* pp. 95–111.
31. *Statutes*, pp. 326–7, 386, 395. For similar difficulties of valuing land in British land-banking, see Melton, *Sir Robert Clayton* pp. 158–78.
32. Pownall, *Administration* p. 242.
33. Ibid. pp. 51, 242–3.
34. See Chap. 3.
35. Pownall, *Administration* p. 241.
36. Ibid. pp. 244–50.
37. SRO, Dartmouth MS, DW 1778/ii/218, Williamos to Dartmouth, 3 July 1766. This was calendared in *The manuscripts of the earl of Dartmouth* (3

vols, Historical Manuscripts Commission, London, 1887–1896) vol. ii, 46 and transcribed in fully in Alan D. Watson, 'A letter of Charles Williamos to Lord Dartmouth, July 1766', *South Carolina Historical Magazine*, 77 (1976) pp. 1–4. Watson did not include the enclosure from Williamos describing his proposed bank (in SRO, DW 1778/ii/762 and Appendix C), possibly because it has been wrongly catalogued as being written in 1776. For Williamos, see *Manuscripts of the earl of Dartmouth* vol. ii, 37, 92 and B. D. Bargar, *Lord Dartmouth and the American Revolution* (Columbia, SC, 1965) pp. 196–7.

38. Ernst, *Money and politics* pp. 106–7, 139–73, 215–41; Rabushka, *Taxation* pp. 657–65, 826–35; Brock, *Currency* pp. 446–62; McCusker and Menard, *Economy of British America* pp. 176–81, 186–8. For capital requirements, see Chap. 1.
39. SRO, DW 1778/ii/218, Williamos to Dartmouth, 3 July 1766.
40. SRO, DW 1778/ii/218, Williamos to Dartmouth, 3 July 1766.
41. Ibid. The emphasis is mine.
42. SRO, DW 1778/ii/218, Williamos to Dartmouth, 3 July 1766.
43. SRO, DW 1778/ii/218, Williamos to Dartmouth, 3 July 1766.
44. John Cannon, 'Petty [*formerly* Fitzmaurice], William, second earl of Shelburne and first marquess of Lansdown (1737–1805)', *ODNB* [https://doi.org/10.1093/ref:odnb/22070, accessed 23 Feb. 2020].
45. CL, Shelburne MS 49/50, L[auchlin] M[acleane] to the earl of Hertford, circa 1765, and Appendix B.
46. L. B. Namier and John L. Brooke (eds.), *History of Parliament: the House of Commons, 1754–1790* (3 vols., London, 1964) vol. iii, 93–4. P.J. Marshall, 'Macleane, Lauchlin [*formerly* Laughlin McLean] (1728/1729–1778), *ODNB* [https://doi.org/10.1093/ref:odnb/40597, accessed 23 Feb. 2020].
47. H. V. Bowen, 'Lord Clive and speculation in East India Company stock, 1766', *Historical Journal*, 30 (1987) pp. 905–20; Kosmetatos, *British credit crisis* pp. 140–54; Lucy Sutherland, 'Sir George Colebrooke's world corner in alum, 1771–1773', *Economic Journal*, 46 (1936) pp. 237–58.
48. Lucy Stuart Sutherland, *The East India Company in eighteenth-century politics* (Oxford, 1962); George K. McGilvary, *East India patronage and the British state: the Scottish elite and politics in the eighteenth century* (London, 2008) pp. 101–2, 140–4, 165; George K. McGilvary, *Guardian of the East India Company: the life of Laurence Sulivan* (London, 2005) pp. 150–65; John Norris, *Shelburne and reform* (London, 1963) pp. 61–2.
49. See Chap. 1.

CHAPTER 3

Specie Banks

Abstract Specie was still seen in this period as the ultimate financial security, and a number of reformers therefore suggested how an imperial paper currency might function in an environment where money invariably drained away from the Americas to Europe. The principles and practices of colonial 'currency finance' and private banking as well as British Exchequer Bills, the Bank of England, Scottish provincial and joint-stock banks and even the Dutch West India Company were all ransacked for ideas about how to support a common circulating medium in the British Empire. All used these ideas to reinforce their wider views about the present and ideal commercial, political and strategic relationship between the imperial metropole and its colonial territories, with proposals ranging from the mundane to the messianic and millenarian.

Keywords Specie • Currency • Alexander Cuming • Richard Jackson • Henry McCulloh

If a currency could not be backed by land it could be backed by liquid assets, such as specie, taxation or commodities. Many economic writers in the British Atlantic insisted that public or private paper notes of any sort could only be sound when they were wholly backed by deposits and convertible on demand into gold and silver coin, which guaranteed that they would maintain a stable price and not be devalued by inflationary

© The Author(s), under exclusive license to Springer Nature
Switzerland AG 2021
A. Graham, *Bills of Union*, Palgrave Studies in the History of
Finance, https://doi.org/10.1007/978-3-030-67677-3_3

over-issues.[1] If there was not enough specie to allow this 'full reserve' banking, then banks might maintain a fractional reserve to meet all contingencies and issue notes upon other secure and relatively liquid assets, such as government securities or commercial paper such as bills of exchange, provided these were 'real bills' arising from genuine commercial transactions rather than 'accommodation paper' without any underlying value and drawn simply for obtaining cash. American colonists were familiar with the practice of 'currency finance' mentioned in the Introduction, whereby paper notes were issued by the colonial assembly and backed by a promise to redeem them with taxes.[2] Though few in Britain would have been prepared to admit it, the various summits of British financial system ultimately rested upon similar foundations, with the Bank of England stabilising the paper currencies issued by local banks with its own notes but relying in turn upon its holdings of government debt to back those notes. All of these elements fed into the proposals which other projectors offered between 1748 and 1768 for an imperial paper currency based ultimately on the redemption of those notes in specie.

British Banks

The British Isles, no less than British America, had faced the problem of inadequate currency in the late seventeenth century, but had found different solutions. The three kingdoms had experienced an increasing shortage of circulating media as specie was drawn overseas by imbalances of trade and to fund British armies overseas, leaving only counterfeit and underweight coins in circulation.[3] Rather than lowering the rating or devaluing coins to reflect this, a decision was taken in 1696 to recall and recoin at full weight all the gold and silver coins in England, restoring the intrinsic value of the coinage and a monetary system based on specie.[4] The money supply was expanded by the creation of the Bank of England in 1694 and its growing circulation of bank notes redeemable in specie on demand, which helped support their value and wider circulation.[5] To bolster its position, competing joint-stock banks were banned in England in 1708, but this did not remove the private banks in London or prevent the formation of country banks of up to six partners in the course of the eighteenth century, which issued their own bank notes that usually enjoyed at least local circulation.[6] It also did not apply in Scotland, which had three chartered joint-stock banks by the 1760s—the Bank of Scotland, the Royal Bank of Scotland and the British Linen Bank—and a large number of unchartered joint-stock banks, as well as several private banks. Together they developed the famed 'Scotch system' of banking, by issuing notes upon mortgages or overdrafts but backing them with specie and circulating them after 1771 by a system of mutual note exchange or clearing.[7] By overcoming the continued shortages of specie in Scotland, this system was one of the factors singled out to help explain its transformative economic development after 1750. By contrast, the banking system of Ireland was seen as a basket case, which had failed to overcome a similar shortage of specie.[8] There was no joint-stock bank capable of stabilising the system until 1783, only a number of private banks which issued their paper irresponsibly and regularly found it impossible to redeem them in specie.

In practice of course the British financial systems rested as much upon the public faith as those of British America. Specie was secure but unproductive and rare, so most of the London and country banks diversified their portfolios to include mortgages on land and reams of commercial and government paper.[9] To provide liquidity it was always possible to draw by bills of exchange upon assets in London, such as Bank of England stock that could be speedily and reliably sold off in secondary markets such as the Stock Exchange. The Ayr Bank in 1769 relied heavily on drawing bills of exchange on London to counteract the problems of locking up most of its capital in mortgages, eventually drawing accommodation paper that shuttled back and forth between London and Scotland to maintain their credit.[10] However, the government securities that made up such a large part of the portfolios of these country banks, and enabled them to circulate such large amounts of paper money, were ultimately backed by public faith in the British state and the political parties that managed it.[11] The same was true of the notes issued by the Bank of England, which country banks held to back their own notes. The Bank of England retained only enough specie to cover its expected demands, which detached note issue from specie and enabled it to ramp up note issues and provide emergency liquidity during crises such as 1772, when a serious contraction in credit bankrupted the Ayr Bank and threatened the rest of the financial system with contagion.[12] Even the specie issued by the Bank to back its notes was ultimately reliant on public faith; as Christine Desan has noted most recently, the fineness and weight of gold and silver coins declined again in the eighteenth century, making them into tokens which retained their value only because by law they continued to pass at their face value.[13]

Projectors contemplating a continental paper currency therefore had a number of British precedents at hand, as well as colonial precedents such as the practice of 'currency finance' noted above. The first bills of credit were issued by Massachusetts in 1690, as an expedient to pay soldiers and contractors during the attack on French Canada, and the success of this measure, as in the case of the land banks, encouraged imitation. Their counterparts in Britain were the Exchequer Bills, first issued in 1696 and intended to provide a circulating medium which would soon be repaid out of taxation.[14] All had a shared origin in the Exchequer Orders issued by the English Treasury after 1667, which provided both public credit and a circulating medium until the Crown broke faith with holders in 1672 by suspending redemption.[15] Memories of this 'Stop of the Exchequer' poisoned subsequent measures in Britain and may help explain the failure of the Exchequer Bills in 1696 to become a circulating medium.[16] As Katie Moore has recently noted, currency finance was no less dependent on public faith—'colonial legislatures gave paper money value, and paper money supported and expressed colonial legislatures' legitimacy'—but necessity meant that the bills of credit became a success.[17]

Multiple models of specie banks and paper currencies were therefore in play, and there was no simple division between British and American practice, since many colonial groups made efforts to adapt English and Scottish models to American conditions. The most ambitious came in 1740 with the plan to incorporate a 'Silver Bank', in opposition to the 'Land Bank' noted in the last chapter. To head off the depreciation and devaluation they expected such a predictably inflationary measure to cause, leading merchants in Boston proposed to form a joint-stock bank to issue £120,000 currency in bank notes, backing them with the specie accumulated from interest payments.[18] By making the notes convertible into specie at fixed rates and periods, emissions of paper would be limited to what the Silver Bank had the assets to back, thereby stabilising the exchange rate and preventing British creditors from being defrauded. It therefore resembled a Scottish joint-stock bank in form and an English country bank in function, but with measures to protect its liquidity in the absence of a close and accessible financial market. What brought the Silver Bank down was not any profound imperial opposition but the political controversy stirred up by the conflict with the Land Bank and the mistrust by British merchants of any scheme granting colonial interests unfettered control of issuing paper money.[19] As a result, the British imperial government was persuaded to ban the formation of any and all joint-stock companies in the colonies without parliamentary sanction. The Silver Bank was therefore caught up in the backlash against the Land Bank, rather than judged on its merits as an orthodox monetary alternative.

Precedents

The various other colonial projects for 'specie' banks in this period have received less attention, but are important as evidence that these models were already in general circulation by the mid-eighteenth century, even in the southern plantation colonies, which have so far usually been overlooked. In 1751, for instance, an anonymous projector in Jamaica produced 'An inquiry into the causes of the present scarcity of money', later published in 1757, which contained an ambitious plan for a public bank to solve similar shortages of currency in the island.[20] First laying out their monetary theory, 'taken from the treasuries of the celebrated Mr Locke on these subjects', the author proposed to issue a devalued coin to take care all small change, and then, 'in imitation of the most celebrated trading nations and following the example of our Mother Country', to erect a bank.[21] The capital of £100,000 in cash would be raised upon a joint-stock in either Jamaica or Britain, while the bank would also have access to a ready supply of specie by handling all the government accounts.[22] Notes for £288,000 could be circulated by this capital fund, on a fractional-reserve basis, to be lent to planters at a high rate of interest that would eventually repay the capital and cover the costs of the bank staff and premises. 'A bank so founded with those privileges and methods of negotiation, subject to just and prudent regulations, and under a wise and impartial direction', the author noted, 'may produce many if not all the happy effects necessary to facilitate the commerce of the country and to relieve the present hardships suffered for want of a due circulation of money.'[23]

Both this bank and the Silver Bank were envisioned as fully incorporated joint-stock banks—the author of the *Inquiry* proposed to obtain a law making the bank 'a body incorporate'—like those in Scotland, but other proposals more closely mirrored the private or country banks proliferating in England. There were several attempts by partnerships or consortia of merchants in New England, New York and Philadelphia to circulate private notes, for example.[24] In Charleston in 1730, in the midst of a serious monetary crisis, a visiting Scottish gentleman and adventurer named Sir Alexander Cuming was badgered by merchants to offer them bills on Britain to allow them to make remittances.[25] He drew about £6000 sterling in bills upon his own credit and lent out the proceeds at interest in the form of his own private notes for over £30,000 currency, forming his own private bank and circulation backed by about £1500 sterling or £10,000 currency in specie and by the bonds he had taken from debtors as security. However, it collapsed disastrously after the bills were returned protested from London and Cuming fled: creditors claimed that when they broke open his chest to recover their money, 'nothing was found in it but some empty boxes, old iron and other rubbish'.[26] Since merchants in Charleston were now left without a convenient currency, a proposal was hatched for a syndicate to form another private bank to circulate about £50,000 currency in private notes, backed only by around £10,000 in colonial paper and lacking any legal tender.[27]

These events drew a response from Cuming which illuminates his attitudes to the question of colonial money and explains the origins of his eventual proposal for a wider imperial paper currency. In a pamphlet aimed at clearing his name, he claimed that securities and other assets worth at least £8000 sterling had been left with his friends to cover the protested bills, that all the creditors had been repaid and that the notes had been a major asset to the merchants, 'as some of them have declared … and in testimony thereof, they desired Sir Alexander to be director of the new bank which they intended to set up in imitation of what they thought to be his measures'.[28] Indeed, his own bank had been superior to the one subsequently set up by the mercantile consortium because he had circulated his notes reluctantly and had made them payable in Spanish silver dollars at a fixed rate of 5s 4d per ounce, close to the market rate in Britain.[29] By contrast, letters from Charleston showed that the merchant syndicate had only got together about £2000 currency in cash for their notes, '[and] although they promise to pay silver, they openly say they will not give any in payments'.[30] As Cuming told the Duke of Newcastle, a leading minister in 1730, such measures were inflationary and would devalue the currency, robbing British merchants, manufacturers and ministries of profits and revenues and making it impossible to defend the frontier.[31] To address these problems he therefore proposed to Newcastle to set up a 'Royal Bank' in South Carolina, based on his own private bank, which would raise £20,000 sterling or £140,000 currency and lend it out as paper notes backed by gold and silver, and therefore 'always upon a solid foundation because payable in the coin or standard of the world, whose value is not so changeable as any other measure of property'.[32] The notes would be exchanged for the £100,000 currency of colonial notes still in circulation, stabilising the money supply, while the remainder would be lent out for productive investment and the interest used to repay the merchants in London who had advanced the capital.

Cuming's plan therefore reflected his personal experiences in South Carolina and his wider views about money and finance. In his memoirs he claimed that in 1719 he had been engaged, 'contrary to his own inclination and judgement, to examine those schemes which were formed by Mr Law', which, if true, might help explain his antipathy to paper money and his preference for specie.[33] After the episode in South Carolina he ended up in Jamaica in 1734 as captain of one of the independent companies sent to quell an uprising by Maroons or runaway slaves.[34] Here, he later claimed, he had proposed a similar measure, using the British pay of the eight companies to support a bank of £10,000 'for the conveniency of that island'.[35] In both cases the financial measures he proposed were part of a wider plan to strengthen imperial authority, standing alongside ambitious hopes to draw the Cherokees into an alliance with the British Empire and rather impractical plans to settle 300,000 Jews in the southern Appalachians to develop the lands, pay off the British national debt and bring about the millennium.[36] Indeed, Cuming was something of a crank, intent on using his expertise to support his obsessions, but in this case his proposals overlapped closely with a range of imperial concerns. In the case of the Royal Bank, for instance, besides saving the province of South Carolina from itself, it would 'keep them from setting themselves up in a state of independency' and support their economic development, 'add[ing] to the riches of Great Britain, to strengthening His Majesty's power, [and] to the increase of His Majesty's revenue'.[37]

The principles and practices of various forms of currency finance and specie banking were therefore in extensive circulation in the British Atlantic by the mid-eighteenth century. Cuming was the first to suggest how these might be scaled up to address the growing problems of commerce, revenue and warfare within a unified empire by the creation of an imperial paper currency. Benjamin Franklin's friend Henry Jackson developed a similar scheme in 1754. A further set of proposals was repeatedly laid before successive ministries by Henry McCulloh in the 1750s and 1760s, with calamitous results, being cannibalised by George Grenville as the basis of the Stamp Act of 1765. The final proposal was submitted in 1767, when the idea of a continental currency was raised for the last time, and represented an unorthodox attempt to subordinate American commerce to British mercantile interests.

Sir Alexander Cuming (1748)

Having proposed the Royal Bank for South Carolina in 1730, Cuming recalled that he then began to ponder the broader applications of his provincial banks, and by 1748 his thoughts had crystallised into a concrete proposal for an imperial bank and paper currency. 'Above eighteen years ago I considered the advantages which might be obtained for Greater Britain by erecting provincial banks in Carolina, New England and elsewhere throughout the British plantations', he noted to one correspondent in June, '[since] I observed the absurdity of making paper notes current in all payments instead of gold and silver specie, when such notes are payable in nothing.'[38] Had he borrowed money in 1730, he might have made his fortune in South Carolina, '[but] I conceived that the power of such a bank would be too great to be trusted in private hands'. Other individuals were now making their own plans though, so he aimed to pre-empt them with proposals for the Treasury in July 1748 for an imperial bank and paper currency 'to preserve the dependency of the British plantations on Great Britain, their mother country, as being their natural and true interest, and as being the surest means to secure their rational liberties and properties against all invaders'.[39] British coins would be made the sole legal coins within British America, and £200,000 would be coined and sent over to be lent out upon land and other securities. The mechanism for this would be 'a provincial bank for all the British plantations in America', issuing bank notes which would be redeemable in coin and a legal tender for the payment of imperial taxes. The effect would be to abolish the circulation of unbacked paper currency and foreign coins, and to ensure that the paper issued never exceeded the amount of money available to back it.

This proposal was further refined the following year, when Parliament voted to grant the New England colonies at least £200,000 in repayment of money laid out for the expedition to capture Cape Breton during the war. Massachusetts used this money to redeem and retire its devalued paper money and successfully return to a currency of gold and silver coin, and a Boston merchant named Otis Little even proposed to use this fund to strike 'a new coin ... calculated for the use of the continent in British America' and suitably devalued to prevent it being exported, but Cuming had even more ambitious aims.[40] The money that Parliament had voted, he told the Treasury in May 1749, was 'sufficient to lay the foundation of a Royal Provincial Bank for the use of the British colonies in America, which will be enabled to abolish all paper money at once, [and] remedy the confusion and obvious abuse of paper credit in those parts'.[41] Rather than receiving cash for their claims, the colonies would receive stock in the bank, with the money itself being lent out at an even higher rate of interest to generate the profits that would enable all the colonies to be repaid with 5 per cent interest after 15 years. To further bolster its capital, Members of Parliament might each invest a further £1000 to carry it on. The proposal was therefore a *piece d'occasion* which dropped the idea of paper currency and aimed to circulate the money in the form of sterling coins, though in every other respect it was merely a continuation of his plans to create an imperial bank and currency to maintain colonial dependence: 'this bank being supposed to be under the immediate inspection of the British Parliament, as a national concern', he said, ' ... the said bank cannot fail to be considered as the source and centre of true credit throughout the British colonies in America.' Indeed, in a Hartlibian gloss, he noted that such banks were widely considered as 'a true philosopher's stone'.[42]

Cuming's plans reached their ultimate refinement during the 1760s. 'A national bank formed on right principles has been evidently distinguished by the wisdom of providence as the true Philosopher's Stone in a well-governed state', he repeated, 'as preferable by far to the richest mines of gold and silver for promoting an honest industry and for increasing the power and wealth of such a state.'[43] Scaling up his plans for the Royal Bank and the Royal Provincial Bank, he set out in his private commonplace book how putting aside £1 million sterling in gold and silver for a British national bank might be used to circulate bank notes for productive investment, with the profits reinvested to increase the original capital, upon true 'patriotick principles'. These included the repayment of the national debt, turning 'Indian and American savages' into local subjects, and the general benefit of mankind, but were primarily 'for improving the British colonies in America and elsewhere, ... and for preserving them at the same time in a natural and easy state of dependency'. The national bank would issue notes for investment across British America, 'for the conveniency of circulation and for promoting useful knowledge, arts and an honest industry, and for increasing the power and wealth of such a well-governed state'. They would also be a legal tender for the payment of taxes but convertible on demand into a specified amount of gold or silver, and the confidence this created would soon enable the bank to circulate three times as many notes as its bullion holdings, on a fractional-reserve basis, producing threefold gains for reinvestment and increasing the capital to £256 million within 40 years, to be used to retire the British national debt. These musings were formalised in 1764 in his memoirs as a plan that £1 million be invested in a 'Royal American Bank' for improving the waste lands in America by circulating notes, with the profits repaying the national debt.[44]

Like so many others, Cuming therefore gradually scaled up his initial proposals to envisage a continental version of his Carolina 'specie' bank from 1730 which would circulate sterling notes throughout British America. 'Which notes', he wrote in the 1748 proposal, 'being payable by the said provincial bank in gold and silver specie on demand, cannot fall under any discount, so long as the managers act agreeably to their several trusts.'[45] His plans therefore most consistently resembled an English goldsmith or country bank, issuing its own notes convertible on demand into gold and silver so as to prevent the fatal excesses of paper currency he had seen in South Carolina in 1730 and before that in France in 1719 during John Law's Mississippi Scheme. Indeed, it was a remarkably consistent element in his proposals, along with the intention to use the bank to advance British imperial power; his plan for a Royal American Bank in 1764, he confessed, was the 'same scheme' he had urged for nearly two decades, and with the same aims, 'of improving the British settlements in America, paying the National Debts of Great Britain, civilising the American savages, adding ten millions of subjects to the Crown of Great Britain and erecting a Bank to facilitate the execution thereof'.[46] Cuming therefore drew repeatedly on his own financial experience in Britain, France and South Carolina to create a continental paper currency to bring about his millenarian imperial and religious vision.

Jackson (1754)

Around the same time that Cuming was hawking around his proposals, the British lawyer, politician and scholar Richard Jackson was in the process of developing his own plan for a provincial bank and paper currency for British America, which, as the last chapter noted, he shared with Benjamin Franklin in March 1754.[47] Whereas Franklin would prove in 1764 to be a fervent supporter of the land bank, Jackson—who was known as 'Omniscient Jackson' for his equally omnivorous scholarship and interests—proposed a continental bank and currency that reflected the monetary orthodoxies and experience of England. For example, while conceding that 'any [circulating] medium is better than none' and that paper notes backed by land, commodities or the public faith might answer, he argued that gold and silver were by far the best ways to make the stable currency necessary for economic development, since they were universally accepted and of fixed value, dampening fluctuations in price. 'A paper currency not convertible at pleasure into money', he demonstrated to his own satisfaction, 'can never become the medium of commerce extended much beyond the power of the legislature that creates it', and proposed instead a 'specie' bank in Philadelphia that would combine the best of both to circulate a stable and secure imperial paper currency.[48] Though it would be based in Philadelphia, Jackson felt that 'a bank of this kind cannot fail in a very short time of becoming the Mint of all N[orth] America, and it will be impossible to prevent their notes from pervading wherever commerce finds its ways in that country'.[49]

Jackson proposed, in other words, to convert the General Loan Office into something not far off the Bank of England, a single bank circulating its notes through British America. The notes now circulated by the General Loan Office on the security of lands would be replaced with a new set of bank notes by the trustees, who would 'be empowered to issue notes payable [in cash and], as our bank notes [are], at sight, and vest in them the other powers given by Parliament to the corporation of the Bank of England'.[50] To facilitate this, an act would be passed in the colonial assembly for its incorporation; Jackson breezily assumed that the statute of 1741 extending the Bubble Act to British America would not apply. A loan would be raised in Britain by subscription to pay off these notes as they were sent home for redemption, the high rates of interest taken in Pennsylvania compensating for the payment of interest in Britain and allowing, by the reinvestment of profits, the trustees in Philadelphia to circulate the notes with their own cash. Jackson predicted that the notes would carry such credit that they would rarely need to be redeemed, so that notes for about £200,000—at least double the £80,000 then circulating in Pennsylvania—could be supported by a fractional reserve of only £40,000 in cash in Britain to answer the bills sent over and a small float in Philadelphia. The primary benefit for Pennsylvania would be the replacement of the land bank notes with a more stable paper currency backed by specie, facilitating remittances, but another benefit would be the wider circulation beyond Philadelphia. Jackson thought that notes for £1 million might be circulated within a few years throughout British America, supported only by a small fund of perhaps £100,000, of which only £10,000 would need to be paid, 'to fortify the credit of the bank, by taking in a subscription like that called here the Bank Circulation'.[51] Other banks might be established along the same lines, but its head-start would make this 'Bank of Philadelphia', as he called it, untouchable.

Jackson therefore proposed to Franklin something diametrically opposed to the land bank, a specie bank reflecting the best of British practices and precedents. As with Cuming, his model was the English goldsmith or country bank, raising its money by private subscriptions and investing it in secure collateral, in this case the mortgages absorbed from the General Loan Office in Philadelphia rather than commercial and government paper, but on the scale pioneered by the Bank of England and its joint-stock counterparts in Scotland. Indeed, it differed remarkably little in practical details from Cuming's millenarian schemes, helping to underline that, whatever the wilder nature of his obsessions, Cuming did at least bring sound financial experience to bear on the problem of imperial currency. The points of difference were small. Both men hoped that their schemes would promote colonial economic development by providing both credit and a stable currency and removing, Jackson said, 'all mischiefs that may now arise for want of a sufficient medium', all without creating political clashes in the Pennsylvania assembly, 'that frequently may otherwise leave animosities that cannot but have pernicious consequences'.[52] However, whereas Cuming went on to add that his bank would cement colonial dependence and imperial authority, Jackson intended wholly to benefit the colonies. It was probably this attitude, rather than the specific nature of Jackson's proposal, which endeared him to Franklin and maybe even helped shape his initial moves against the Currency Act in late 1764. 'I have always been inclined against a paper currency, I mean a legal tender paper currency', Franklin told Jackson, not wholly honestly, after a meeting with the other colonial agents at the Board of Trade to discuss the act, 'and though I conceive difficulties occurring for want of it at times, I am satisfied they are to be removed by a bank ... and (if insurmountable objections should arise in the way of a public bank), I wish it were a provincial one by private bankers on a sufficient foundation'.[53] Franklin's first plans were therefore for something resembling Jackson's specie bank, and only later did he bring forward his own land bank.

McCulloh (1751–1765)

For all their focus on imperial authority and colonial dependence, both Cuming and Jackson at least had some concern, like Franklin and Williamos, for promoting the economic development of the colonies. This was more than could be said for their counterpart Henry McCulloh, yet another disappointed imperial adventurer who offered proposals for a continental currency to a series of British politicians and officials between 1757 and 1764. McCulloh had been one of the largest landowners in North Carolina in the 1740s and the surveyor of quit-rents for the Carolinas, but had backed the wrong horse in a political clash with other land speculators and was driven out of the colony in 1747, near the end of the War of the Austrian Succession (1740–1748).[54] Perhaps unsurprisingly, he was far more concerned even than any other writer to develop a continental currency that would extend British imperial authority, both fiscal and military, as part of his wider plans for the government of the colonies. Few of these plans were ever taken up and those that were, like the Stamp Act and Sugar Act, had disastrous consequences. During this period though 'his was an articulate voice in Britain on the subject of the American colonies and the themes of imperial regulation and colonial reform', Bumsted has noted, '… [and] his writings nevertheless provide an important illustration of how the American Empire could be viewed by knowledgeable men in the 1750s, as well as indicate the sorts of motivations which prompted such scrutiny'.[55] Those plans for an imperial currency have not been studied in any systematic way, but they demonstrate a particularly acute diagnosis of the problems that colonial currencies posed for warfare and taxation in British America and an uncompromising determination to advance British fiscal and military interests without much reference to colonial sensibilities.[56]

Like other commentators, McCulloh's views were, Bumsted has noted, 'a direct extension of his own experiences', in this case of North Carolina during the 1740s.[57] These experiences had demonstrated the limits of imperial authority, the problems of governors more sympathetic to the colonial interests than imperial direction and the irresponsibility of colonial assemblies in issuing paper money. Bumsted argues that McCulloh recognised the need to accommodate colonial interests, but his proposals suggest that this was actually a pragmatic concession to help implement them rather than reflecting any genuine sympathies for the colonial position. McCulloh took his cue instead from the closer and more cohesive imperial control which the French Crown supposedly exercised over its own colonial territories, comparing the Board of Trade in London unfavourably with the Council of Commerce created in Paris in 1714 'to demonstrate that the plan or system of all offices is to be considered as a piece of clockwork, which by its springs directs the wheels in motion'.[58] In 1751 he was already writing to the Board of Trade to propose a range of taxes on imports, sugar, rum and paper that would create a central fund in America for the use of the imperial government, the fore-runner of his ill-fated proposals in 1764 for an imperial stamp tax and sugar duty.[59] In 1757 and 1758 he called the attention of the ministry and the public to the haphazard emission of paper money by individual colonies, '[which] hath often had a public and a general effect and greatly injured the trade and commerce of this kingdom', to be addressed by a continental paper currency 'as a medium or standard in the intercourses of trade'.[60] His main concern though was for the creation of an imperial militia that could operate throughout the colonies alongside regular troops in the service of imperial interests, funded by these new duties and paid in this new paper currency.[61]

McCulloh was therefore one of the earliest to recognise the problems for imperial fiscal and military state formation created by separate paper currencies under the control of individual colonies, whom he argued were the root of the problem. Not only was their control of the money supply a presumptuous usurpation of the royal prerogative and a means of cheating British merchants and manufacturers, but the inevitable over-issues and consequent devaluations meant that there was 'no regular course of exchange between one province and another'.[62] The bills of credit from individual colonies were 'liable to large discounts in the neighbouring provinces, to the great obstruction and detriment of all manner of business, public and private', creating additional costs for the British government.[63] To raise revenue and pay troops it would be necessary to suppress colonial currencies entirely, as the British government had already done in New England in 1751, and replace them with a shared continental paper currency, 'for if at any time hereafter we unite the colonies, so as to make them all concur and act together for the goods of the whole', he argued, 'the having different kinds of currency will … lay them under great difficulties in the payment of their quotas or in paying the troops which may be sent from one colony to the aid and assistance of another.'[64] Unlike the other writers, McCulloh therefore cared very little either for the economic development of British America or for the interests of British merchants, but focussed instead upon the consequences of the current currency system for imperial military and fiscal power.

To address this McCulloh offered up to three options, depending on his audience. The first was to maintain the *status quo*.[65] The second, proposed in 1757, was to use his stamp tax and sugar duties to raise about

£60,000 per year and 'establish and incorporate a Bank at London, by the name, style and title of the Bank of America'.[66] Merchants and financiers in London could subscribe at least £1 million in specie and sit on the Court of Directors, with committees of correspondence in New York, Williamsburg and other places 'for the greater and more regular dispatch of business'.[67] The bank would use its cash to back an emission of sterling bank notes as a common paper currency for the payment of taxes and troops and for remitting money back to Britain. Indeed, he hoped that the credit and credibility of these new notes would encourage individual colonies to take up and cancel their own notes, 'which are from their uncertain and fluctuating nature of great disservice to the credit, trade and commerce of the colonies'.[68] They could then set up loan offices or land banks 'in the manner which has been practiced in Pennsylvania', offering these notes to borrowers rather than issuing their own. Investors in Britain would need only to raise about £100,000 in cash as a fractional reserve to redeem these notes in specie, and in return would enjoy the profits of lending out £1 million sterling at 6 per cent interest. Like Jackson's proposal to Franklin in 1754 but on an even grander scale, this proposal therefore used the Bank of England to suggest how a counterpart might exercise similar monetary functions in British America.[69] In this case, however, the bank would be based in London rather than Philadelphia, thereby ensuring that imperial authority remained wholly undiluted.

The third option and the one which McCulloh consistently favoured was to create a new type of financial instrument called an 'Exchequer Bill of Union', based on the Exchequer Bills already described earlier.[70] Somewhere between £150,000 and £300,000—the amount varied— would be printed as an imperial paper money for the payment of British and colonial troops in British America, in small denominations but carrying 6 per cent interest.[71] As they matured they would be repaid in the cash, initially from the British Treasury but eventually by imperial poll taxes and stamp duties that would raise between £50,000 and £120,000 per year, with measures being taken to ensure that emissions did not outstrip the means of redemption and cause devaluation. McCulloh likewise hoped that it would encourage colonies such as New York to exchange their own bills of credit and the colonial taxes which backed them for the Exchequer Bills of Union, 'which may enable them to pay off their present bills of currency; and after the use of one medium of currency is better understood, the charter governments will likewise see it their interest to enter into the same course of proceeding'.[72] Rather like Macleane, another imperial official frustrated at how the colonies had abused a good idea, he therefore proposed to adapt the American process of 'currency finance' and its English precedents into a mechanism for imperial unity by creating an imperial paper currency under responsible British control which would drive all others out of the market.

Some form of continental paper currency was therefore a consistent component in McCulloh's programmes for imperial reform, joining together the new taxes to be raised and the new troops to be maintained, as well as enabling ancillary aims such as making gifts and consolidating alliances with Native American tribes.[73] When he offered his scheme once again to George Grenville, the prime minister, in 1764 it differed little from his prior proposals either in scope or in scale, and now adduced the recent wartime experience to support his case.[74] 'The want of a fund applicable to the use of America produced many and fatal effects before the commencement of the late war', he concluded, ' ... [and] the necessity of introducing one uniform currency or medium of trade in all the colonies is self-evident.'[75] By tightening up customs and reducing smuggling, it would be possible to raise at least £30,000 per year by taxes on wine, sugar, rum and molasses to circulate £500,000 in Exchequer Bills of Union, at a rate of 4 per cent interest, replacing the devalued bills of credit issued by the individual colonies. 'The colonies from their partial interests and connections will give all the opposition in their power to this or any other matter which can be proposed for the general good of the subject', he admitted, 'but if paper Bills of Credit are at present absolutely necessary as a medium in trade, the issuing of Bills of Union under the sanction of Parliament will ... be of infinitely more service to the public and to the trading interest than of allowing the colonies to issue bills of currency as a tender in law.'[76]

Unfortunately for McCulloh's proposals and for imperial authority in British America, Grenville adopted the plans for imperial taxation, customs enforcement and cutting off colonial bills of credit, but not the plan for an imperial currency to replace them and enable colonists to pay the new imperial taxes.[77] As protests against the stamp tax and sugar duties increased in volume, McCulloh submitted a further proposal diagnosing the issue; 'there is not specie in most of the said colonies to enable the people settled there to pay in specie the several duties required from them', he wrote, '... [and] those sudden revolutions in trade and in government, without substituting anything as a medium in the course of payments, will have a fatal tendency, both with respect to the public concerns of the colonies and to trade and commerce.'[78] Some form of unified colonial government under an imperial aegis was still necessary and so was a continental paper currency that could correct the worst excesses of the provincial bills of credit, and McCulloh therefore repeated his plan to emit Exchequer Bills of Union and make them legal tender for all imperial taxation and spending, in order '[to] obtain a circulation'.[79] A new wrinkle was the proposal to use the stamp and sugar taxes to fund a lottery that would raise about £4 million or £5 million to make an imperial coinage for British North America, 'to be transmitted there for the payment of the troops and other contingent charges'.[80] It would be coined at a fineness or alloy one-quarter below the English market value—not to prevent exportation, since it would circulate by its intrinsic weight, which was the usual reason for this exercise, but simply to provide a silver specie which might, presumably, ease the payments of imperial taxes now made payable only in silver by weight.[81] 'By this means, America will be supplied with silver specie so as to answer all payments, both of a public and of a private nature', McCulloh noted '... [and] strengthen the hands of the Administration in enabling them to settle and improve our new acquisitions in America.'[82]

The various iterations offered by McCulloh between 1751 and 1765 of his plan for a continental paper currency therefore shared a broad resemblance. Like Williamos and Macleane, he was primarily concerned with maintaining British power in North America, but he saw this mainly in administrative rather than commercial terms. Whereas others wanted to back the currency with specie to protect British merchants, McCulloh saw this as a way to reduce the costs and inconvenience of the intercolonial exchange and to support improved revenues and defence. He was firmly pragmatic, though perhaps not ultimately practical, in his aims and addressed issues which were becoming increasingly troubling to the British government. The single point it had in common with these and all other proposals for an imperial paper currency is that it was never enacted. By 1767 and Pitt's second ministry, all the proposals were essentially dead in the water, and even Franklin had abandoned his plans to focus simply on the repeal of the Currency Act of 1764, even managing to persuade most of the British merchants that allowing colonial assemblies to resume their emission of bills of credit would help restore trade. On 11 May 1767 they presented a petition to Parliament pressing for the repeal of the act.[83] All seemed to be settled, '[but] two days later', notes Ernst, when the Chancellor of the Exchequer Charles Townshend presented his package of imperial fiscal measures to Parliament, 'the incubus of Franklin's former scheme for a British land bank in the colonies arose to plague the negotiation and the wreck the chance of any immediate repeal'.[84] This gave rise to the final proposal considered here, in many ways the most original and ambitious.

TOWNSHEND (1767)

For reasons apparently reflecting little more than personal pique, the former prime minister George Grenville suggested reviving Franklin's continental land bank as a further revenue measure. Townshend was forced to counter with his own proposals, which one agent described to the colonial assembly of South Carolina as plans 'to establish a Loan Office in the respective provinces with a power of issuing paper currency carrying an interest', to be issued on good security and with the interest supporting imperial government.[85] Whether or not Townshend seriously intended to revive a version of Franklin's land bank and its continental currency is now unclear, since his death in September 1767 cut off its progress. McCulloh's son Henry, the agent for the colony of North Carolina, reported back two weeks later that the ministry was still exploring three options for a continental currency for America. One was his father's proposal for Exchequer Bills of Union; the second was for a Bank of America 'as an appendage to the Bank of England, and to supply us with Bank notes', closely resembling McCulloh's proposal from 1757; the third, '(and I think the most probably and eligible), to take the affairs of the colonies out of the hands of Parliament and place them in their old channel ... by repealing the restrictive acts' and better regulating individual colonial emissions.[86] Townshend's papers suggest though that these were not the only proposals he had to hand. A memorial written about this time entitled 'Proposals for establishing paper currency for North America' offered a plan that developed even further the principles and practice of a specie bank, but in a new way, and based even more directly on Scottish banking and monetary practices and even Dutch commercial precedents.

The 'Proposals' suggested chartering a joint-stock company called the Company of Merchants Trading in Exchanges, to be backed by at least £100,000 in cash. Its Court of Directors in London would appoint 'Chambers of Management' in the colonies, who would issue sterling notes of five shillings or more that could be exchanged at branches in North America or Britain for gold or silver coin after a year. All coin would pass by weight at the market rates in London, preventing colonies from tweaking the ratings of coin. The colonies would also be required to give up their currencies and to adopt sterling as their unit of account. The notes issued by the company could be used in turn 'to discount bills or notes of hand; lend money on bonds, mortgages or other securities they shall think proper in the said colonies, at an interest of six per cent per annum; ... [and] open cash accounts ... and all monies paid to be in the Company's notes', providing a full range of financial services specialised for colonial merchants and manufacturers requiring access to short-term credit for liquidity. Besides selling bills of exchange upon London for the benefit of colonial merchants seeking to make remittances, the Company would also effect intercolonial transfers of money between the Chambers of Management in each colony by 'instruct[ing] the said chambers to draw bills on one another and thereby establish a course of exchange in the colonies'. Even inland exchanges such as that between London and Edinburgh required management, but this process would have simplified remittances by putting them in the hands of a single institution which would be big enough to dominate the market and set rates for others to follow.[87]

As a bank, the Company would therefore have most resembled neither the Bank of England, which was restricted to a single site in London until it was permitted to open branches in 1825, nor the private banking partnerships of England, Scotland and Ireland, but the Scottish joint-stock banks, especially the Bank of Scotland, Royal Bank of Scotland and British Linen Company.[88] The other Scottish provincial banks were unincorporated and operated under deeds of co-partnership, but were closer to these three in size and scope than to English country banks, having large numbers of shareholders and similar management structures.[89] Unlike in England, where private banks shunned mortgages in favour of more liquid assets, the Scottish banks also tended to make extensive advances upon land, as the Company proposed to do.[90] As noted above, they pioneered the overdraft or 'cash account' system which the Company proposed to employ.[91] By contrast, the usual method of raising money in English commercial and country banking was to draw and discount bills of exchange. The method of intercolonial exchange by circulating notes between the different chambers also mirrored the practices of Scottish joint-stock banks, who were pioneering in the 1760s and 1770s the practices of branch banking.[92] These branches traded on the capital of the main office and allowed money to be moved around the country either by a cheque or by inland bills of exchange. By contrast, the English country banks still relied on complex webs of bilateral agency relations with other local banks, which drew bills on each other to effect transfers.[93]

The Company also reflected Scottish joint-stock banking practice in its organisational and administrative structure. The small size of most English country banks made for informal management, whereas the Scottish joint-stock banks imitated the Bank of England and developed an early separation between the Court of Directors and the professional administrative staff.[94] Branches or agencies were usually placed under consortia or syndicates of local merchants, providing the bank with local knowledge about the credit and reputation of customers while ensuring that the head office ultimately remained in control.[95] A similar measure was planned for the Company, with the Chambers of Management or Direction in each colony having several directors holding stock, but named by the Court of Directors in London 'and subject to their orders'. Colonial interests only had the right to choose a director in London, one per chamber, but as they were to constitute no more than a third of the Court of Directors, the power of those colonial interests would always have been outweighed by those of the metropole. The Company was therefore structured to maintain British influence even at a distance. What the Company proposed, in other words, was to apply Scottish branch banking to the British Atlantic, using their experience of managing specie-backed paper money and banking services across large spaces lacking both coinage and credit. Indeed, when the first British imperial banks were formed for Ireland and the Empire in the 1820s and 1830s, this was precisely the model they adopted, keeping their head offices in London and forming dependent branches in the colonies which were closely subordinated to central direction.[96]

Finally, among the most interesting and ambitious provisions was that the chambers in the colonies would offer bills of exchange on London to colonists to enable them to remit funds home. 'To enable the chambers of the colonies to make remittances to England for retiring their bills of exchange and notes', it added, 'they shall be at liberty to purchase and remit and ship, to Great Britain only, any of the enumerated goods of the said colonies.' These were the goods which the navigation acts only allowed to be shipped to Britain and included British America's most profitable exports, including sugar, tobacco, cotton, indigo and ginger.[97] With a capital far outweighing that of most merchants, as well as an unrivalled commercial presence and quite literally a licence to print money, this would have made the Company the largest single trader in British America, able to set the price on its most valuable commodities and to dominate trade. It would therefore have closely resembled the Dutch West India Company or *Geoctrooieerde Westindische Compagnie*, still a going concern in the mid-eighteenth century, which had made strenuous efforts to monopolise the plantation trade of Dutch America.[98] This comparison is lent weight by the decision to call the Company's local boards of directors in British America 'chambers', presumably inspired by the urban chambers or *kamers* set up by the West India Company and its East Indian counterpart in the seventeenth century. The *kamers* had a degree of independence but were subject to the court of directors, the *Heeren XVII* in the case of the West India Company, who were elected by the individual chambers. The author of the 'Proposal' thus drew on Dutch as well as Scottish commercial practices to develop an institutional framework for an imperial paper currency, this one firmly subordinated to British commercial interests.

Conclusion

The death of Townshend in September 1767 ended any lingering chances that a form of continental currency might be brought in, either in the form of a land bank or as a specie bank. As noted above, even Franklin had backed away from his proposal by this stage and was focussed on repealing or merely relaxing the Currency Act of 1764 to allow a return to the *status quo*. The brief window between 1764 and 1767 when some sort of continental currency seemed both essential and possible, leading to a number of proposals that were in circulation though not necessarily in dialogue with each other, therefore rapidly closed. As the previous chapter noted, some of those were based upon the colonial experience of land banks, but adapted their principles and precedents to meet their specific ambitions for imperial authority and colonial development. The various plans put forward between 1748 and 1767 for an imperial paper currency backed by specie were developed in a similar way. Experiments in the British Isles and British Atlantic with banking went back over a century, and projectors drew on these precedents to develop proposals that served their wider aims for the British Empire in the mid-eighteenth century, the messianic and the millenarian as well as the more mildly mundane.

Notes

1. See Chap. 1
2. For overviews, see Ferguson, *Power* pp. 3–24; Ferguson, 'Currency finance', pp. 153–80; Brock, *Currency* pp. 17–49; Nettels, *Money supply* pp. 250–7; Newell, *Dependency to independence* pp. 127–35
3. Dickson, *Financial revolution* pp. 46–57; Craig Muldrew, 'Wages and the problem of monetary scarcity in early modern England', in Jan Lucassen (ed.), *Wages and currency: global comparisons from antiquity to the twentieth century* (Berne, 2007) pp. 392–409; Kleer, *Money, politics and power* pp. 54–63, 186–202; Horsefield, *Monetary experiments* pp. 13–28, 73–90.
4. Dickson, *Financial revolution* p. 349; Kleer, *Money, politics and power* pp. 117–33, 171–81; Horsefield, *Monetary experiments* pp. 28–70; Desan, *Making money* pp. 361–7.
5. Desan, *Making money* pp. 295–329; J. H. Clapham, *The Bank of England: a history* (Cambridge, 1945) vol. i, 21–2, 144–50; Kleer, *Money, politics and power* pp. 29–49; Pressnell, *Country banking* pp. 159–61; J.A.S.L. Leighton–Boyce, *Smiths the bankers: 1658–1958* (London, 1958) p. 51; Horsefield, *Monetary experiments* pp. 125–43.
6. For country banks, see Desan, *Making money* pp. 376–81, 388–404; Pressnell, *Country banking* pp. 4–11, 136–59, 190–234; Leighton-Boyce, *Smiths* pp. 7–33, 139–259. For goldsmith-banks, see Peter Temin and Hans-Joachim Voth, *Prometheus shackled: goldsmith banks and England's financial revolution* (Oxford, 2013) pp. 31–72; Iain S. Black, 'Private banking in London's West End, 1750–1830', *London Journal*, 28 (2003) pp. 29–59. For proposals along these lines, see Horsefield, *Monetary experiments* pp. 144–52.
7. Checkland, *Scottish banking* pp. xvii–xviii, 91–134; Horsefield, *Monetary experiments* pp. 152–4; Goodspeed, *Legislating instability* p. 7; Munn, *Scottish provincial banking companies* pp. 81–5, 97–8, 220–37.
8. L. M. Cullen, 'Landlords, bankers and merchants: the early Irish banking world, 1700–1820', *Hermathena*, 135 (1983) pp. 25–43; Walsh, *South Sea Bubble* pp. 125–42, 163–80; Horsefield, *Monetary experiments* pp. 154–5; Rowena Dudley, 'The failure of Burton's Bank and its aftermath', *Irish Economic and Social History*, 40 (2013) pp. 1–30; Marie-Louise Legg, 'Money and reputations: the effects of the banking crises of 1755 and 1760', *Eighteenth-century Ireland/Iris an dá chultúr*, 11 (1996) pp. 74–87. Similar criticisms were levelled at the English system, but only from the 1790s onwards: Pressnell, *Country banking* pp. 441–510.
9. Dickson, *Financial revolution* pp. 228–43, 415–69; Pressnell, *Country banking* pp. 75–125, 162–80, 284–439; W.T.C. King, *History of the London discount market* (London, 1972) pp. 1–34; B. L. Anderson,

'Money and the structure of credit in the 18th century', *Business History*, 12 (1970) pp. 85–101; Eric Kerridge, *Trade and banking in early modern England* (Manchester, 1988) pp. 76–81; Leighton-Boyce, *Smiths* pp. 27–8, 46–8, 58–60, 67–135; Temin and Voth, *Prometheus shackled* pp. 84–95, 125–47; Clapham, *Bank* vol. i, 104–57.

10. Kosmetatos, *British credit crisis* pp. 83–122; L. M. Cullen, 'The Scottish exchange on London, 1673–1778', in S.J. Connolly, R.A. Houston, and R.J. Morris (eds.), *Conflict, identity and economic development: Ireland and Scotland, 1600–1939* (Preston, 1995) pp. 38–9; Jacob M. Price, 'The Bank of England's discount activity and the merchants of London, 1694–1773', in Ian Blanchard et al. (eds.), *Industry and finance in early modern history* (Stuttgart, 1992) pp. 99–100; Checkland, *Scottish banking* pp. 124–8; Goodspeed, *Legislating instability* pp. 93–109.

11. Dickson, *Financial revolution* pp. 341–406; Nathan Sussman and Yishay Yafeh, 'Institutional reforms, financial development and sovereign debt: Britain, 1690–1790', 66, 4 (2006) pp. 906–35; John Wells and Douglas Willis, 'Revolution, restoration and debt repudiation: the Jacobite threat to England's institutions and economic growth', *Journal of Economic History*, 60 (2000) pp. 418–41; David Stasavage, 'Partisan politics and public debt: the importance of the "Whig Supremacy" for Britain's financial revolution', *European Review of Economic History*, 11 (2007) pp. 123–53; Gary W. Cox, 'War, moral hazard and ministerial responsibility: England after the Glorious Revolution', *Journal of Economic History*, 71 (2011) pp. 133–61; and ultimately D. C. North and B. R. Weingast, 'Constitutions and commitment: the evolution of institutions governing public choice in 17th century England', *Journal of Economic History*, 49 (1989) pp. 803–32.

12. For the Ayr Bank, in particular, see Kosmetatos, *British credit crisis* pp. 175–249; Sheridan, 'Crisis of 1772', pp. 161–86; Cullen, 'Scottish exchange', pp. 38–9; Price, 'The Bank of England's discount activity and the merchants of London, 1694–1773', pp. 99–104; Checkland, *Scottish banking* pp. 128–34; Desan, *Making money* pp. 308–20; Goodspeed, *Legislating instability* pp. 93–109; Richard Saville, *Bank of Scotland: a history, 1695–1995* (Edinburgh, 1996) pp. 156–66. For the credit crisis, see above n. 10.

13. Desan, *Making money* pp. 376–85.

14. Dickson, *Financial revolution* pp. 365–72; Aaron Graham, 'Credit, confidence and the circulation of Exchequer bills in the early financial revolution', *Financial History Review*, 26 (2019) pp. 63–80; Kleer, *Money, politics and power* pp. 203–13; Clapham, *Bank* vol. i, 38–9; Horsefield, *Monetary experiments* p. 124; Desan, *Making money* pp. 339–41.

15. Dickson, *Financial revolution* pp. 43–5, 365; Horsefield, *Monetary experiments* pp. 114–24, 144–54; Desan, *Making money* pp. 245–54, 274–81; C.D. Chandaman, *The English public revenue, 1660–1688* (Oxford, 1975) pp. 224–8; Jonathon Scott, '"Good Night Amsterdam": Sir George Downing and Anglo-Dutch statebuilding', *English Historical Review*, 118 (2003) pp. 334–56.
16. J.E.D. Binney, *British public finance and administration, 1774–92* (Oxford, 1958) pp. 127–31; Dickson, *Financial revolution* pp. 372–9; Richard Kleer, '"A new species of money": British Exchequer bills, 1707–1711', *Financial History Review*, 22 (2015) pp. 179–203; S.R. Cope, 'The Goldsmids and the development of the London money market during the Napoleonic Wars', *Economica*, 9 (1942) pp. 180–206; Kleer, *Money, politics and power* p. 213; Clapham, *Bank* vol. i, 53–6, 64–72.
17. Moore, 'Blood that nourishes', pp. 23–36, quotation on p. 25; See also Ferguson, *Power* pp. 7–10.
18. See Chap. 2.
19. Newell, *Dependency to independence* pp. 225–34; Brock, *Currency* pp. 195–6; Ernst, *Money and politics* pp. 34–6.
20. BL, Add MS 30163, 'An Inquiry into the causes of the present scarcity of money and the bad consequences of it to this island, with some proposals for a remedy wherein the scheme of a Public Bank is offered, Jamaica, Anno 1750'.
21. BL, Add MS 30163, 'Inquiry' ff. 2r, 37v.
22. BL, Add MS 30163, 'Inquiry' ff. 39v–40v.
23. BL, Add MS 30163, 'Inquiry' ff. 43r.
24. Ernst, *Money and politics* pp. 34–6, 122–9, 137–9, 255; Brock, *Currency* pp. 49–53; Andrew Mcfarland Davis, 'A Connecticut land bank of the eighteenth century', *Quarterly Journal of Economics*, 13 (1898) pp. 70–84; Andrew Mcfarland Davis, 'The merchants' notes of 1733', *Proceedings of the Massachusetts Historical Society*, 17/37 (1903) pp. 184–208; Bruce P. Stark, 'The New London Society and Connecticut politics, 1732–1740', *Connecticut History Review*, 25 (1984) pp. 1–21; Perkins, 'Conflicting views', pp. 17–20; Newell, *Dependency to independence* pp. 183–7, 197–202; Wright, *Origins* pp. 33–6, 60–2. See also a later effort in Philadelphia in 1766: Wright, *Origins* p. 61; Ernst, *Money and politics* pp. 122–9.
25. The following is based on TNA, CO5/361 ff. 133v–134r, 'Humble Memorial of Sir Alexander Cuming' to the Duke of Newcastle, 11 July 1730 and ff. 135r–v, 'Copy of a letter from a merchant in Carolina [to Cuming]', (undated but circa 1730), as well as Sir Alexander Cuming, *The case of Sir Alexander Cuming Bart, truly stated, in relation to merchants in So[uth] Carolina* (London, 1730) and *Boston Daily News–Letter* no. 187

(23 to 30 July 1730), 'Extract of a letter from South Carolina, dated June 12, 1730'. This work has benefitted from my conversations with Ronald Michener. For the monetary crisis, see Brock, *Currency* pp. 113–27; Ernst, *Money and politics* pp. 122–9.
26. *Boston Daily News-Letter* no. 187 (23 to 30 July 1730), 'Extract of a letter'.
27. TNA, CO5/361 ff. 135r–v, 'Copy of a letter'; Cuming, *Case* pp. 10–12. Further details are given in *The Journal of the Commons House of Assembly of South Carolina* ed. J.H. Easterby et al. (14 vols, Columbia, SC, 1951–89) vol. i, 309–10. For Newcastle's dismissive response, see TNA, SP 36/19/1 f. 14r, Newcastle to Cuming, 8 June 1730.
28. Ibid., pp. 4, 5–8, 9.
29. Ibid., p. 9.
30. TNA, CO5/361 ff. 135r–v, 'Copy of a letter'.
31. TNA, CO5/361 ff. 133v, 'Humble Memorial'.
32. TNA, CO5/361 ff. 133v–134r, 'Humble Memorial'; Cuming, *Case* pp. 10–12.
33. BL, Add MS 39855 (Memoir of Sir Alexander Cuming, circa 1764) ff. 13r–14r.
34. BL, Add MS 39855 f. 25r.
35. BL, Add MS 39855 ff. 31r–32r.
36. Gordon Goodwin and Philip Carter, 'Cuming, Sir Alexander, second baronet (1691–1775)', *ODNB* [https://doi.org/10.1093/ref:odnb/6891, accessed 23 Feb. 2020].
37. TNA, CO5/361 f. 134r, 'Humble memorial'.
38. JRL, Egerton of Tatton MS, EGT/2/6/2/66, Sir Alexander Cuming to Samuel Hill, 28 June 1748. I have not been able to find any surviving copies of these proposals for New England and other colonies.
39. Daniel Lysons, *The environs of London, being an historical account of the towns, villages, and hamlets, within twelve miles of that capital, interspersed with biographical anecdotes* (2 vols., London, 1811) vol. i, part. ii, 765; BL, Add MS 32714 ff. 107r–v, Cuming to Newcastle, 26 January 1748.
40. Brock, *Currency* pp. 244–334; Rabushka, *Taxation* pp. 576–80; Malcolm Freiberg, 'Thomas Hutchinson and the provincial currency', *New England Quarterly*, 30 (1957) pp. 190–208. For a copy of Little's proposal, see Otis Little, 'Proposals for a new currency in America' (13 July 1748) in BL, RP 380/2, Reel 2 No. 1035. I believe the original is in the John Carter Brown Library, Providence, Rhode Island, MSS Codex Eng. 33 but have been unable to confirm this.
41. TNA, CO 323/12 ff. 9r–v, 'The Humble Memorial of Sir Alexander Cuming', 9 May 1749.
42. TNA, CO 323/12 f. 9v, 'Humble Memorial'.

43. NL, Ayer MS, MS 204, Commonplace book of Sir Alexander Cuming (circa 1760–7), and Appendix I.
44. BL, Add MS 39855 ff. 39r–40r.
45. Lysons, *Environs* vol. i, part. ii, 765.
46. BL, Add MS 39855 ff. 39r–40r.
47. W. P. Courtney and J.-M. Alter, 'Jackson, Richard, (1721/2–1787), politician', *ODNB*, 23 Sept. 2004 [https://doi.org/10.1093/ref:odnb/14546, accessed 23 February 2020]; Namier and Brooke (eds.), *HOP 1754–90* vol. i, 669–72.
48. Van Doren, *Letters and Papers* pp. 47–52.
49. Ibid., pp. 53–4.
50. Ibid., pp. 50–1.
51. Ibid., p. 52.
52. Ibid., p. 53.
53. *Franklin Papers* vol. xi, 175–7, Franklin to Jackson, 13 April 1764; Ernst, *Money and politics* pp. 79–82.
54. J.M. Bumsted, 'A forgotten prophet: Henry McCulloh and reform of the British Empire', *Canadian Review of American Studies*, 13 (1982) pp. 1–12; Ernst, *Money and politics* p. 78; Mattie Russell, 'McCulloh, Henry', in William Powell (ed), *Dictionary of North Carolina Biography* (6 vols, Chapel Hill, NC, 1979–2001) vol. iv, 133.
55. Bumsted, 'Forgotten prophet', pp. 1–2.
56. For brief mentions of his plans for a continental currency in prior historiography, see Ibid., pp. 9–11; Sosin, 'Imperial regulation', p. 176n; Ernst, *Money and politics* pp. 78–80, 97, 99, 204; Bullion, *Great and necessary measure* pp. 65, 108–9, 211, 287n1; Shannon, *Indians and colonists* p. 68.
57. Bumsted, 'Forgotten prophet', pp. 3–9; Shannon, *Indians and colonists* pp. 64–8; BL, Add. MS 11514, '[An] Essay, pointing out the best way of improving the trade and manufactures of America, by Henry McCulloh; addressed by him to the Earl of Halifax. Dat. London, 10 Dec. 1751', ff. 13r, 90v–94v. For North Carolina and paper currency, see Brock, *Currency* pp. 106–13, 428–45; Ernst, *Money and politics* pp. 82–7.
58. BL, Add MS 11514, 'Essay' ff. 13r; Henry McCulloh, *Proposals for uniting the English colonies on the continent of America, so as to enable them to act with force and vigour against their enemies* (London, 1757) pp. 3–6.
59. Bullion, *Great and necessary measure* pp. 64–76, 104–10, 287n1. Many of these thoughts were then repeated publicly six years later in McCulloh, *Proposals for uniting the English colonies* pp. 1–8, 22, 30–6, and again in a cut-down form in 1761 addressed to the Earl of Bute in Henry McCulloh, *Miscellaneous representations relative to our Concerns in America, submitted in 1761-to the Earl of Bute* (London, 1905 [1761]) pp. 1–6, 12–22.

60. McCulloh, *Proposals for uniting the English colonies* pp. 17–20; BL, Add MS 32874, f. 308r, McCulloh to Newcastle, 26 September 1757, and ff. 310r–v, [Proposals for Exchequer Bills of Union]; TNA, PRO 30/8/97, 'Draft of a bill for creating and issuing bills of credit under the denomination of *Exchequer Bills of Union* for the general use of His Majesty's colonies on the continent of America' (circa 1757) ff. 173r–v.
61. Ibid., pp. 16, 27–9, 36–7; BL, Add MS 32874, f. 310r [Proposals]; TNA, PRO 30/8/97 f.173v.
62. Ibid., pp. 17–20, 29; This was also mentioned briefly in McCulloh, *Miscellaneous representations* p. 12.
63. BL, Add MS 32874 ff. 310r–v [Proposals]; TNA, PRO 30/8/97 f. 173r–v. For the problems of losses on British remittances, see Nettels, *Money supply* pp. 179–201; Shy, *Toward Lexington* pp. 240–4, 336–7.
64. McCulloh, *Proposals for uniting the English colonies* pp. 17, 20, 29. This was also mentioned briefly in McCulloh, *Miscellaneous representations* p. 12. For the difficulties that were experienced remitting customs revenues around British America for the use of the army, see Chap. 1 and Barrow, *Trade and empire* pp. 218–20.
65. McCulloh, *Proposals for uniting the English colonies* p. 23.
66. McCulloh, *Proposals for uniting the English colonies* pp. 23–6.
67. Ibid., p. 24.
68. Ibid., pp. 25–6, 37.
69. See Chap. 2.
70. McCulloh, *Proposals for uniting the English colonies* p. 22. BL, Add MS 32874 ff. 310v–312r [Proposals]; TNA, PRO 30/8/97 'Draft of a bill' ff. 173v–175v.
71. BL, Add MS 32874 ff. 310v–311r, 312r–v [Proposals]; McCulloh, *Proposals for uniting the English colonies* pp. 22–3.
72. BL, Add MS 32874 f. 312r [Proposals].
73. McCulloh, *Proposals for uniting the English colonies* p. 29.
74. HL, STG Box 12/28, McCulloh 'General Thoughts with respect to such Regulations as are humbly conceived to be necessary in America and in the Islands in the West Indies lately ceded to us by France' (1764). There is a copy in Bullion, *Great and necessary measure* pp. 211–19. This probably represented the gist of the draft bill 'for creating and issuing bills of credit under the denomination of Exchequer Bills of Union for the general use of His Majesty's colonies in America', which McCulloh submitted to Grenville with the plan for his stamp duty when he came into power in July 1763 and described to Grenville as resembling the proposals sent to Halifax in 1755 'with some alterations [that] will answer the end proposed at this time': *The Grenville Papers: being the correspondence of Richard Grenville ... [and]*

George Grenville ed. William James Smith (4 vols, London 1852–3) vol. ii, 374n; Ernst, *Money and politics* pp. 78–9, 99–100.
75. HL, STG 12/28 'General Thoughts'. This had been given greater prominence as well in his letter to Bute: see McCulloh, *Miscellaneous representations* pp. 11–12.
76. HL, STG 12/28 'General Thoughts'.
77. Henry McCulloh, 'General thoughts, endeavouring to demonstrate that the legislature here in call cases of a public and general concern, have a right to tax the British colonies; but that with respect to the late American Stamp Duty Bill, there are several clauses inserted therein which are very exceptionable, and have, as humbly conceived, passed upon wrong information', in Jack P. Greene, '"A dress of horror": Henry McCulloh's objections to the Stamp Act', *Huntington Library Quarterly*, 26 (1963) pp. 253–62; Bumsted, 'Forgotten prophet', pp. 11–12; Bullion, *Great and necessary measure* pp. 2, 65–70, 104–10.
78. Greene, '"Dress of horror"', pp. 258–9.
79. Ibid., pp. 258–60.
80. Ibid. This bore a certain resemblance to Otis Little's plan in 1748 for an imperial coinage: see above n. 40.
81. See Chap. 1.
82. Greene, '"Dress of horror"', pp. 259–60.
83. Greene and Jellison, 'Currency Act', pp. 498–500; Sosin, 'Imperial regulation', pp. 189–90; Ernst, *Money and politics* pp. 100–18.
84. Ernst, *Money and politics* p. 118; Griffin, *Townshend moment* pp. 127.
85. See the letter of Garth to the Commissioners of Correspondence, 13 June 1767, in Joseph W. Barnwell, 'Garth Correspondence (continued)', *South Carolina Historical and Genealogical Magazine*, 29 (1928) pp. 228–9. See also Ernst, *Money and politics* pp. 118–20; Greene and Jellison, 'Currency Act', p. 499; Sosin, 'Imperial regulation', p. 190.
86. *Colonial and State Records of North Carolina* (26 vols, 1886–1907, Winston, NC) vol. vii, 517 Macleane was still under-secretary of state for the Southern Department at this point, not leaving his position until June 1768.
87. For the management by Scottish banks of the London–Edinburgh inland exchange of sterling bills, see Cullen, 'Scottish exchange', pp. 29–44; Checkland, *Scottish banking* pp. 32–3, 62–6; Saville, *Bank of Scotland* pp. 30–2, 42–4, 79–80, 106–7, 151–3, 188–92, 254, 262–3; Munn, *Scottish provincial banking companies* pp. 121–6, 184–91.
88. For the Scottish system, see n. 7.
89. Munn, *Scottish provincial banking companies* pp. 103–6, 152–6; Checkland, *Scottish banking* pp. 111–18.

90. For Scottish banks, see Checkland, *Scottish banking* pp. 62–6, 124–34; Saville, *Bank of Scotland* pp. 111, 112, 116, 128–30, 139–40, 263–4, 267–9. Munn notes though that provincial banking companies (with the exception of the Ayr Bank in 1772) did not tend to invest in mortgages or heritable bonds: see Munn, *Scottish provincial banking companies* pp. 126–7. For English banks, see Pressnell, *Country banking* pp. 344–85; Leighton-Boyce, *Smiths* p. 61; Temin and Voth, *Prometheus shackled* pp. 125–47.
91. Checkland, *Scottish banking* pp. 62–76; Pressnell, *Country banking* pp. 284–321; Munn, *Scottish provincial banking companies* pp. 115–21.
92. Checkland, *Scottish banking* pp. 96–104, 116, 127–8; C. W. Munn, 'Banking on branches: the origins and development of branch banking in the United Kingdom', in P.L Cottrell, Alice Teichova, and Takeshi Yuzawa (eds.), *Finance in the age of the corporate economy* (Aldershot, 1997) pp. 37–51; Munn, *Scottish provincial banking companies* pp. 173–82; Saville, *Bank of Scotland* pp. 109–10, 167, 179–86, 266–7.
93. Pressnell, *Country banking* pp. 126–35, 190–3; Margaret Ackrill and Leslie Hannah, *Barclays: the business of banking, 1690–1996* (Cambridge, 2001) pp. 15–33; Leighton-Boyce, *Smiths* pp. 36–45, 60–3, 139–259.
94. Checkland, *Scottish banking* pp. 26–33, 196–203; Saville, *Bank of Scotland* pp. 81, 302–6; Munn, *Scottish provincial banking companies* pp. 159–71.
95. See n. 89.
96. A.S.J. Baster, *The imperial banks* (London, 1929) pp. 49–122; Geoffrey Jones, *British multinational banking, 1830–1990* (Oxford, 1993) pp. 13–62; Lennox Barrow, *The emergence of the Irish banking system, 1820–1845* (Dublin, 1975) pp. 61–197.
97. McCusker and Menard, *Economy of British America* pp. 47, 161, 179.
98. Cornelis Ch. Goslinga and Maria J. L. Van Yperen, *The Dutch in the Caribbean and in the Guianas, 1680–1791* (Assen/Maastricht, 1985) pp. 12–20.

CHAPTER 4

Conclusion

Abstract Ultimately none of the proposals for an imperial paper currency were adopted, but their importance was nevertheless profound. They show that even in the mid-eighteenth century it was already becoming possible to conceive of a currency system or monetary union that could unite British America and overcome its political, economic and military problems. They failed to become reality only because the political will was lacking. The proposals were therefore the first stage in a prolonged, halting and largely iterative process of currency reform after 1776 in both the new United States and the British Empire, which each adopted programmes of monetary union as the military, fiscal and commercial problems of the circulating medium first diagnosed in the mid-eighteenth century made themselves felt.

Keywords Money • Monetary union • American Revolution • British Empire

There was no direct connection between any of the proposals put forward between 1748 and 1768, on the one hand, and the creation of a continental currency by Congress in May 1775 and the incorporation of the Bank of North America four years later on the other. Yet they were nevertheless of great importance. They show that even in the mid-eighteenth century it was already becoming possible for several writers to conceive, largely independently, of a continental or imperial currency as a solution to some or even all of the military and commercial problems that now faced the empire. In 1748, only a crank such as Sir Alexander Cuming thought a continental currency either desirable or practical, but by 1764 a number of grave, sober and experienced imperial reformers were insisting that it was essential, even if their solutions were inevitably filtered through their own aims, priorities, interests and experience of currency and finance. These projects formed an essential part of the wider move towards imperial reform and uniformity in the mid-eighteenth century. They were also merely the initial stages in iterative processes of monetary union enacted, with varying degrees of success in the United States, Britain and the British Empire after 1775. This concluding chapter explores why none of these proposals were adopted, what impact they might have had and the wider conclusions which can be drawn from these proposals about the process of monetary union in the mid-eighteenth century.

FAILURES

The failure to enact any of the proposals for a continental currency during this period was not because imperial officials and politicians were inherently opposed to such grandiose projects. As was noted at the start, in 1763 the Board of Trade was willing to sponsor a range of measures designed to cement imperial unity within the British Atlantic, 'a coherent British vision of western empire', as Max Edelson has put it, 'that sought to displace settlers as meaningful agents in favour of a regulated system of colonisation orchestrated from London'.[1] Measures to populate and develop the new territories had mixed success. In Canada and the Floridas, it proved difficult to attract settlers.[2] In the Ceded Islands in the British Caribbean, lands were rapidly sold for development, but only after substantial concessions and compromises.[3] There were also rare triumphs, such as the successful surveying and negotiation of the proclamation line along the Appalachians between 1763 and 1774, even if in practice it could not be enforced and therefore proved redundant.[4] Military and fiscal measures were applied uniformly across British America and even in some cases the British Caribbean as well, demonstrating the willingness of the British government to embrace grand imperial projects. The failure to create an imperial paper currency before 1775 reflected the lack of interest from colonial groups, a similar apathy among British interest groups, and the substantial costs of such proposals for the imperial government when compared with their limited benefits.

Firstly, colonial interests in the British Atlantic showed no sign of wanting an imperial or continental currency. Franklin was an outlier, as the muted responses in 1754 to his plans at Albany for imperial political union showed, and even he soft-pedalled his proposals for an imperial land bank after 1764 in the face of apathy or even outright opposition from colonial interests.[5] Many colonists argued for expanding the supply of cheap credit with more paper money, and others cautiously supported a more limited expansion of the circulating medium by the careful emission of a paper money securely backed by taxes. However, since most colonies already possessed proven systems of currency finance and land banks, which were under their political control and accountable to colonial rather than imperial needs, few apparently saw any advantage to an imperial land bank or continental currency. Intercolonial commerce could be handled by the remittance of coin or sterling bills of exchange or by the circulation of colonial paper beyond its original colony, as in the backcountry and the continental seaboard between New York and Virginia.[6] Ernst and others have shown that colonial groups therefore bent all their efforts towards securing the repeal of the Currency Acts of 1751 and 1764. They initially made some limited headway, until the earl of Hillsborough, who had drafted the Currency Act as president of the Board of Trade in 1764, was made southern secretary of state in 1767 and repeatedly blocked their efforts.[7] Colonists then focussed either on securing exemptions, as in New York in 1770, or discovering loopholes. Once Hillsborough surrendered the seals of office in 1773, the way was open for the Currency Act of 1773, which formalised these loopholes and permitted colonies to issue bills of credit that were not legal tender but which could be taken for colonial taxes, and serve in every other respect as currency for the colonies.[8]

The fact that colonial groups showed no interest in an imperial currency meant that it could only be enacted by the British imperial government, at its own initiative or under pressure from metropolitan interests, as in the case of the Sugar Act of 1764, which partly reflected the influence of the West India lobby.[9] However, British merchants were not interested in a continental currency either. Their initial efforts in 1764 were aimed at restricting colonial paper entirely.[10] By 1766 this had weakened, but since most still dealt directly and bilaterally with correspondents in major colonial centres and their respective hinterlands, apparently few saw any major benefit from a continental currency whose chief selling point over a better-regulated system of colonial paper currencies was its ability to facilitate intercolonial capital transfers.[11] From their perspective, the Currency Act of 1764 and the amending act of 1773 served their ends just as well. The only party that would really have benefited from a continental paper currency in the British Atlantic was thus the imperial government itself, but, as earlier chapters noted, a set of practices such as 'army sterling' had evolved by 1764 to deal with the issue.[12] These expedients were makeshift, inconvenient and mutually incompatible, but they did at least work.[13]

Thus, the question that faced British ministries between 1748 and 1767 was whether the undoubted but limited benefits of erecting a continental currency in British America outweighed the undoubted and potentially unlimited expenses involved, both financially and politically. As previous chapters have shown, most of the proposals envisioned a high degree of imperial intervention as ministers set the quotas for bank note issues and loans, which would have made them the target for imperial and colonial complaints about inadequate or excessive emissions. Most of the land bank proposals anticipated the imperial government suppressing the colonial banks that were already in existence, and Franklin and Pownall even argued that counterfeiting the notes should be made a capital crime, both measures sure to cause violent opposition if implemented. All the land bank proposals would also necessarily have involved the imperial government and its agents carrying on suits against defaulters and foreclosing on their lands. This was a procedure which caused an immense deal of resentment when used to recover arrears of imperial quit-rents and other taxes, with colonists often making use of their control of local courts to obstruct the process.[14] Indeed, even the Pennsylvania Loan Office had difficulties recovering its debts and was repeatedly forced to roll them over rather than confront borrowers over their default.[15] Finally, although the profits arising from circulating paper money at interest was a major selling point in many proposals, which noted that it might be used to fund imperial expenses, the allocation of the profits of the existing land banks proved a common point of contention between colonial assemblies and governors in the 1760s and 1770s, and this would only have increased under an imperial land bank or loan office disposing enough money to do away with colonial assemblies entirely.[16] Enacting any of the proposals would therefore have exacerbated existing political tensions while offering only limited benefits over the existing fiscal-military infrastructure.

Consequently, the only circumstance in which an imperial paper currency might have emerged before 1775 was in the unlikely but not impossible case of the British government finding it so useful that it would ride roughshod over colonial objections or fund the necessary costs itself. Only two options were plausible, and it is probably no accident that they were the only ones which received sustained attention from the British government and imperial officials before 1767. Franklin's proposal could be expected to create the least resistance among colonists because it surrendered imperial control over monetary policy, and for this reason would probably never have been enacted by the British state. By contrast, McCulloh's proposal promised direct advantages for imperial military and financial unity, and might have defused colonial objections by operating largely alongside the existing colonial system and—initially—at British rather than colonial expense.[17] What circumstances could have led to it being enacted, and what might have been the consequences for the development of British America after 1763? The value of exploring such hypotheticals is not that they necessarily prove anything, but they serve as a productive intellectual exercise, in this case for considering what would have been necessary for a continental currency to emerge in 1764 and whether those factors were in place when it did in 1775. As Niall Ferguson has suggested his survey of counterfactual history, 'if we want to say anything about causation in the past without invoking covering laws, we really have to use counterfactuals, if only to test our causal hypotheses'.[18]

Hypotheticals

It is plausible to imagine a moment in the Seven Years War when the ministry were confronted by a financial crisis for which the Exchequer Bills of Union appeared the ideal solution, perhaps, for example, if the army in North America had suddenly found itself without any specie for paying either the local contractors or even the soldiers themselves. After all, a similar financial emergency had led to the unlikely creations of the Bank of England and the Land Bank in Britain between 1694 and 1696.[19] As I have shown elsewhere, running out of money for the army was a constant concern for the contractors hired by the Treasury for remitting money to North America.[20] 'You cannot depend on any further remittances of specie', they told their agents in April 1759, for instance, '[as] this kingdom is so exhausted of both gold and silver that we are fairly told at the Treasury it is better to submit to the loss than to drain it further.'[21] The only recourse was to attempt to raise it out of the money circulating in North America, but their agents noted the difficulty they faced finding any, and used all their political influence in New York and Pennsylvania to encourage these provinces to make additional emissions of paper money in 1759 and 1760 to meet their urgent need for a local circulating medium.[22] Sir Jeffrey Amherst, the British commander, commented in May 1759 that this measure was 'the only means left to enable me to carry on the intended operations with the necessary vigour and despatch'.[23] Had the provinces refused to cooperate, Amherst and the army would have put very strong pressure on the British government to find other expedients. A desperate ministry, which was already throwing money at the war, might therefore perhaps have been persuaded to look again at McCulloh's most recent plan for his Exchequer Bills of Union, the version he had submitted in September 1757.

As noted in the last chapter, this envisaged the creation of £300,000 sterling in Bills of Union, in denominations from 5s to £20, and carrying 4 per cent interest. The agents of regiments in North America would issue them to the troops, and the interest would be paid out of the general credit of the Exchequer until Parliament could pass the necessary imperial taxes to pay the interest and redeem the bills at maturity in 1769.[24] This would probably immediately have run into the same issues encountered in England in the 1690s when the first efforts were made to circulate Exchequer Bills as currency.[25] Of uncertain value, based only upon the general credit of the Exchequer rather than a fixed revenue stream, and not redeemable for cash except at maturity, the first effort in 1696 was a disaster, as only about £160,000 of the £1.5 million authorised entered circulation. Subsequent tranches offered better terms, enough to make them into instruments for short-term credit, but they never became a circulating medium. The concurrent circulation of Bank of England notes made them superfluous, and the inclusion of interest made them unwieldy as circulating instruments, since their value depended on calculating the dates of transfer and the interest due.[26] The same would probably have occurred with the Exchequer Bills of Union in 1759, except that the rate of interest which McCulloh proposed was also so far below prevailing rates in British America—about 6–8 per cent by law, and frequently higher in reality—that the Bills would have been useless as investments unless they were accepted by colonial merchants at such high rates of discount as to render them uneconomic as a circulating medium.[27]

Consequently, the only way to make the Bills viable would probably have been to remove the interest altogether and allow them to circulate as bank notes, backed by the promise to redeem them in specie. Printed and sent over to North America, the Bills would have helped to preserve what little specie remained for the payment of local suppliers, who often refused to receive anything but gold or silver coin.[28] 'You would lose here by gold or dollars being sent, yet I am convinced £100 in either of these articles would induce them to do more than £1000 in paper', reported one agent of the provision contractors from the Virginia backcountry in August 1759, for example, '[as] the old misers take more delight in telling over the pieces of gold or silver than twice the quantity of paper. The first question they ask me is, if I will give them any hard cash?'[29] The Bills of Union would also probably have circulated at a steep discount, at least initially, until the ministry took the logical step of passing an act allowing them to be received for imperial taxes to encourage their circulation, and adopting the same expedient of a fund to redeem the Bills in specie on demand, on the principles that kept the Bank of England notes and Exchequer Bills in Britain in circulation.[30] How many Bills of Union would have been issued is impossible to say, but it is hard to envisage the imperial government limiting themselves to the mere £300,000 proposed by McCulloh once the convenience of issuing the Bills in lieu of specie became clear. In the real world, the profit which the public obtained from the process of remittance turned into a loss in 1759 and 1760 as the premiums on specie rose, and this would probably have encouraged the British government to issue more rather than continue to absorb this loss.[31] Indeed, at a moment when the ministry was borrowing vast sums at high rates of interest, the temptation to print large tranches of Bills of Union for British America for nothing and to rely upon paying them back later—ironically, in much the same manner as the colonial assemblies themselves—would probably have become irresistible.[32]

In this hypothetical situation, the British Atlantic would therefore have exited the Seven Years War in 1763 with a large amount of imperial paper money in circulation, probably at moderate rates of discount, and a correspondingly reduced amount of the colonial paper currency. It is hard though to see how British imperial policy would have been much different. There would still have been immense financial pressure to impose taxes upon British America, not least to help redeem the large amount of Exchequer Bills of Union issued.[33] The Bills themselves would probably have continued to circulate, at least among imperial taxpayers, soldiers and their suppliers. It is even likely that something akin to the Currency Act of 1764 banning colonial currencies would have been passed, now not only to protect the British merchants but also to prevent them competing with the Bills of Union remaining in circulation. British merchants might also have looked more favourably upon the Bills, as they did on colonial currencies after 1766, since they were immune from fluctuations in the rate of exchange. Indeed, it is highly likely that ministries would have come under pressure from both imperial and colonial interests to continue issuing Bills of Union in order to maintain the money supply of the colonies. Other episodes such as the brief rearmament during the Falklands Crisis in 1770 and then the credit crisis in the British Atlantic of 1772 would probably have led to further emissions, first as military readiness was stepped up and then as colonists pressed for more paper money to overcome this shortage of credit, which was met in reality after 1772 at the level of individual colonies as they increased their emissions.[34]

Colonists would therefore have faced the same contentious demands from British ministries for revenue, but now payable in a reasonably abundant imperial paper currency. This probably still would not have been enough to avoid outright conflict during the 1760s and 1770s. The scholarship on the Stamp Act and the Currency Act notwithstanding, the problems of paying this tax without an adequate circulating medium was only one of the causes of resistance, which also reflected resentment at the principle of taxation without political representation after the strenuous efforts made by the colonies during the Seven Years War.[35] At best they might have moderated the political impact of the Currency Act of 1764, but Greene and Jellison point out that 'compared to other issues in the debate between Britain and America, the Currency Act was not one of the explosive ones'. By 1774 it was no longer an issue, and its precursor had anyway been in effect since 1751 in New England, where the revolution broke out, without more than minor complaints.[36] Overall therefore it is likely that the Exchequer Bills of Union, had they been implemented, would still have done little to prevent conflict erupting in the British Atlantic after 1763.

However, the existence of the Exchequer Bills of Union in 1774 might have been sufficient to disrupt the outbreak of violence and to affect its course. As the British regime found after the Glorious Revolution in 1688, and as the Continental Congress was shortly to discover, the creation of any public debt dependent on the regime was a powerful force for loyalty, since the value of that debt rested on the survival of that regime.[37] As Alexander Hamilton noted in 1795, he had supported the assumption of state debts by the federal regime in part due to 'its tendency to strengthen our infant government by increasing the number of ligaments between the government and the interests of individuals'.[38] Or, as one British writer put it in 1776, convening loyalist assemblies and causing them to put paper into circulation, backed by British guarantees but redeemable at a distant date, 'would make it the interest to every individual in America that England should gain the victory, just as the public debts after the [Glorious] Revolution here confirmed the revolution'.[39] Had there been many hundreds of thousands of pounds of imperial currency in circulation in 1774 at the outbreak of revolution, backed by imperial taxes and held by large numbers of people who in reality ended up supporting the Patriot cause, this would probably have helped to shift some of those towards the British camp. Given the tenuous unity the Congress displayed at this early stage, the effect might have been to deter a wholesale revolt and instead produce a more scattered and much less unified set of uprisings. They would have been more vulnerable to suppression and perhaps even enabled Britain to meet its aim in 1774 of isolating New England from the rest of British America, not least because British imperial forces would now also have had immediate access to an independent source of finance for military action which they did not in reality.

Histories of the outbreak of the American Revolutionary War note, in particular, the slow reaction by the imperial government to the formation of the first Continental Congress in September 1774.[40] Partly this was a question of policy, since the British ministry was in the midst of a general election called to endorse the confrontational policy adopted towards America, but it also reflected the delays as Thomas Gage, the commander-in-chief of British forces in North America, referred back to Britain the question of reinforcements. By September he was already warning that the British forces were inadequate for the task of suppressing the anticipated violence and had to be augmented before they could be used; 'if force is to be used at length', he told Dartmouth privately in October, 'it must be a considerable one ... for to begin with small numbers will encourage resistance and not terrify, and will in the end cost more blood and treasure.'[41] Some small reinforcements were brought in from the garrisons in Quebec and New York, but Gage was forced to wait for Dartmouth to despatch further troops from the British Isles, which was deferred until the winter storms had abated.[42] These delays gave the Patriots a vital window to consolidate their power in New England by seizing control of militias and arsenals and making preparations for taking to the field with their own army, as Gage watched in frustration.[43] One way to break this up would have been to mobilise support on the spot by raising loyalist forces able to provide immediate reinforcement. Indeed, Gage told Dartmouth that 'the regiments are now composed of small numbers and irregulars will be very necessary in this country, many of which of one sort or other I conceive may be raised here', as he had done in the Seven Years War, and several loyalist associations were formed in Boston over the winter before Dartmouth wrote back rejecting the idea.[44] Had Gage been relieved of the need to refer all questions back home and instead been able to issue paper money on demand, to recruit the British regiments and raise a force of loyalists for an immediate strike against the Patriots, he might at least have been able to decapitate the movement and begin the conflict on British terms in late 1774 rather than on Patriot terms in early 1775.

The failure to create an imperial or continental currency between the first proposal in 1748 and the final one in 1767 therefore probably had a small but significant impact on the course of the 1760s and 1770s. The British government saved itself a great deal of time and money, and avoided enacting measures that would probably only have further riled up colonial interests. Only McCulloh's plans for Exchequer Bills of Union stood even a small chance of being passed, largely because they would sit on top of the existing structures rather than replacing them, and would have been effected at least at first at Britain's expense. Under these conditions they would probably also have rapidly evolved into something more directly resembling a government paper money rather than their original model, but would still have done little to prevent a confrontation occurring at some point in this period. That confrontation however might have been more scattered and less cohesive than in reality, perhaps more closely resembling the experiences of Latin American independence between 1808 and 1826, and reflecting the strongly centrifugal tendencies which survived even during the American Revolution. Instead of fighting in many ways a traditional conflict of nation-states and national armies, which was ended with a diplomatic settlement in 1783, Britain and the British Empire would instead have been drawn into a long-running and debilitating series of violent insurgencies and rebellions which would probably have further destabilised other parts of the empire such as Ireland and the British Caribbean and invited repeated foreign interventions.

Monetary Unions

Working through both the reasons for the failure of these proposals and the highly specific set of circumstances under which they might have been enacted helps, in turn, to understand the choices facing both the Patriots and the British Empire in 1775 as they confronted the problems of warfare. In particular, it suggests that the emergence of the Continental dollar as a common currency at the outbreak of the conflict occurred because the very specific set of conditions just noted had arrived. As the main authority coordinating the Patriot war effort, one which involved the transfer of men and money across provinces into key strategic theatres, the Congress now acutely felt the need for a common currency which could facilitate this process. Although relying on the individual colonies for funding, it was patently impossible to pay the Continental Army in the paper notes of individual colonies, which had uncertain value outside their original colonies and were in any case rapidly becoming devalued as the colonies stepped up their own emissions. Neither was it possible to rely on paying troops in specie, which was being exported to pay for weapons and supplies in Europe. The only viable solution was to create not just a new monetary unit of account to replace sterling, the Continental dollar, as a common reference of value, but also a shared medium of exchange, the Continental notes, which could then circulate alongside the colonial currencies to support Continental military needs across the Thirteen Colonies without interrupting the tenuous alliance between them. In principle the paper dollar was tied to the value of the silver dollar, but in practice there was no possibility of conversion, and by deferring their promise to redeem the paper money the Congress was able to issue the vast amount of paper needed to sustain the war effort. Indeed, without any independent powers of taxation, this saved them from irrelevance versus the state governments; 'as long as paper money lasted, it allowed Congress to assume and discharge the main burdens of the war', Ferguson noted, '[thereby] conferring upon the central government a power and freedom of action out of character with its constitutional position.'[45]

Politics and necessity therefore came together to support the establishment of the Continental currency in 1775, and the result was something very close to McCulloh's plan for Exchequer Bills of Union, reflecting a common solution to the fiscal problems of waging war upon a continental scale.[46] Because of this necessity the Congress, however, yielded to temptation and issued greater and greater amounts of paper, $400 million by nominal value between 1775 and 1779, by which point it had become so devalued as to become almost useless as a medium of exchange. Between 1779 and 1781 the war effort was virtually demonetised, as the Congress demanded resources in kind or transferred the costs to the individual states. In 1781 the Congress then gave their support to the formation of the Bank of North America, a plan of the financier and treasurer Robert Morris.[47] Like the Bank of England, this private joint-stock bank would manage Continental debt issues and, on this security and its capital of $400,000—about £90,000 sterling—circulate paper bank notes that passed current across the Thirteen Colonies. The scheme therefore echoed not just an earlier proposal by Alexander Hamilton in 1779 but McCulloh's and Jackson's proposals in 1757 and 1754 for a 'Bank of America' to issue notes in the colonies as a common currency. Morris was the first person though in a position to bring his proposal to fruition, which enabled the Continental Congress to exploit the defeat of Cornwallis at Yorktown in August 1781 and to claim victory. McCulloh's prediction in 1757 that his plan would be 'of infinite service to the colonies and the proprietors of the bank' was therefore proved right.[48]

By the same token, as the political necessity which had supported these unpopular centralising measures dissipated after 1783, the financial system and the Continental currency regressed almost to familiar pre-war conditions. The capacity of the Congress to issue its own money was threatened by the declining status of the Bank of North America, now increasingly under the sway of mercantile and financial interests in Philadelphia and unwilling or unable to continue its risky position as the nation's banker.[49] The dollar remained a common unit of account, but Congress faced competition as states reasserted their right to create paper money, either by currency finance or by land banks. As Schweitzer and others have shown, their objectives were sometimes to provide a monetary stimulus to repair their shattered economies, but some states such as Rhode Island once more used it as an opportunity to pay off their wartime debts in devalued local currency. 'The situation', Ferguson noted, 'could have been regarded as normal; the various states were re-enacting their particular experience with paper money in colonial times.'[50] The Confederation Congress was now facing the same problems as the British imperial government, of managing an overarching military and financial system dependent on interstate transfers without a common medium of exchange, and a fluctuating set of state currencies outside their political control. Grubb has argued that as the Constitutional Convention met at Philadelphia in 1787, bankers were pushing for a ban on these state currencies to profit from the monopoly this would give the Bank of North America, which had recently defeated an effort by Pennsylvania to withdraw its charter to support its own paper money. Michener, Wright, Schweitzer, Ferguson and others argue more persuasively that state emissions had largely been discredited by devaluation, and the uneven repayments of Continental debts in devalued currency threatened to undermine the political unity of the Confederation.[51] To this should also now be added the problems that this system posed for a national military and fiscal system which many Federalists envisaged.

Consequently, the measures adopted after 1787 to establish the United States dollar as the dominant unit of account and medium of exchange should be seen not just as an effort to address the damaging economic and political consequences of state currencies but also as a key adjunct to the viable federal fiscal-military state being created at the same time. As recent work has shown, the Federalists at the Constitutional Convention favoured the construction of a more centralised military and financial system, to bolster national unity, assert federal authority in the unsettled territories beyond the Appalachians and defend against European encroachment.[52] Elements included a national system of customs duties and revenue officers, funding a federal army, navy and public debt, and a land office system for selling off federal lands for settlement, all of which depended on a common unit of account and medium of exchange. Like the British imperial state, the American federal administration had to wrestle with the new states to achieve this. The United States dollar coin was created and given a specified weight and fineness.[53] A small amount of coin was minted, but the bulk of the federal contribution to the money supply was in the form of paper notes issued by the new Bank of the United States, denominated in dollars, backed by its holdings of government securities and foreign specie, and legal tender for federal payments and debts across the United States.[54] When the Bank was not in existence, between 1811 and 1816, and again after 1836, Treasury Notes were issued which served the same purpose as money. States were banned from issuing any further paper and gradually abandoned using their own currency ratings in favour of the United States dollar, but continued to create paper money for economic development at arm's length by chartering their own joint-stock banks. As recent work has emphasised, these notes filled much the same role as former issues of colonial paper, fluctuating in price depending on the reputation of the underlying bank, though various central clearing-house systems in New England after 1818 and New York after 1853 helped to provide regional stability and a degree of monetary union. However, because they were no longer legal tender, they could no longer interfere directly with the operation of the land, debt and fiscal-military systems under federal authority.

The American monetary union, as it gradually evolved after 1775, was therefore a political creation, formed as a necessary adjunct to the creation of a unified fiscal-military system capable of resisting British power. The magnitude and immediacy of the threat provided the Continental Congress with political capital necessary for overriding the vast array of vested interests who would otherwise have opposed the Continental dollar and which had deterred British reform in the wake of 1764. As these factors ebbed and flowed, so did the power to create a federal paper currency which would knit these elements together and facilitate fiscal and military measures. Only when the United States faced another national emergency in the 1860s was there once more sufficient political capital to override the status quo and put a government currency into circulation, and to begin to phase out the issue of notes by private banks.[55] There were therefore substantial continuities in North America across the century from the 1760s to the 1860s, as successive regimes wrestled with the problems of managing military and fiscal systems upon a continental scale in the face of powerful local vested economic and political interests.

The proposals for a continental currency in British America after 1748 were likewise the first stages in the development of the British imperial monetary union during this period, which culminated after 1870 in the rise of the pound sterling as a global currency. In Britain itself, monetary union after 1764 remained—and remains—incomplete. Although Bank of England notes had widespread circulation and largely retained their value, even during the suspension of convertibility into specie between 1797 and 1821, it was not until 1834 that they were made legal tender in England and formally became a paper currency.[56] In the light of the parliamentary Bullion Committee of 1810, Britain was not only returned to a specie standard but formally adopted the gold standard in 1816, reducing its silver and copper coins to the status of token coinage. Country banks and the new joint-stock banks which began to emerge after 1825 were required to redeem their notes on demand in coin, and the Bank Charter Act of 1844 began the process of suppressing the issue of competing notes by these banks. However, Ireland and Scotland existed after 1817 in the same indeterminate position in relation to the British government as the

American states did in relation to the federal government. On the one hand, the pound sterling was the dominant unit of account, the Bank of Scotland, for example, having abandoned the Pound Scots before 1707, though it remained in use elsewhere until the 1740s.[57] British gold and token silver coinage were legal tenders, and the Bank of England notes were a widely accepted medium of exchange though these were not, and are still not, a legal tender. However, banks in Scotland and Ireland also issued—and continue to issue—their own sterling notes, which mirrored American state bank notes insofar as they were denominated in the national currency and had to be payable in a legal tender such as coin or, in practice, Bank of England notes.

Successive British ministries had therefore decided that the political difficulties of achieving full monetary standardisation and consistency across the United Kingdom outweighed the economic gains. Neither were they much more successful on the colonial periphery. As earlier chapters outlined, the departure of the United States in 1783 did not take away the need for an imperial currency. British North America and the British Caribbean remained, and the empire also continued to grow in size, increasing both the complexity of imperial administration and the need for a common unit of exchange or currency. Less was achieved than in the United States, because the economic position of the components of this monetary union were more disparate, its vested interests were more diverse, its political power was weaker and the necessity for monetary union appeared less urgent. Indeed, the prevailing impetus behind this programme, beyond a general effort to tidy up and standardise economic, political and social norms across Britain and the empire, was administrative convenience and a desire to correct the anomalies resulting from decades of wartime expedients and the haphazard annexation of foreign colonies and their monetary systems during the Revolutionary and Napoleonic Wars.

The process was driven largely by the Treasury, which remained frustrated at the complex accounting needed to cope with paying the British troops and officials overseas.[58] '[We] consider it as being highly expedient that [we] should avail [ourselves] of the present period of peace … for introducing a fixed and uniform medium of exchange for all transactions connected with the public service', the Treasury Minute of 11 February 1825 noted, 'in the place of the various fluctuating and anomalous currencies which have been created under the pressure of temporary emergency or with views of local and peculiar expediency … and which have been productive of much private and public inconvenience.'[59] An Order in

Council fixed the rate of foreign coins in sterling terms across the empire as a first step towards replacing the colonial currencies with sterling as their common unit of account and the foreign coins with sterling coins as their common medium of exchange. In practice however it was a failure.[60] The ratings were ignored in British North America, which was tightly integrated into the American economy, and the territories of the East India Company were exempted and remained on their own monetary standard. The Order had most effect in the colonies in Australia and the Cape of Good Hope, which were all economically isolated and lacked much political autonomy. In the Caribbean it was strongly resisted, because the region was also integrated with the American economy and because it overvalued the silver dollar at 4s 4d sterling per dollar, disrupting established monetary norms. A supplementary Order in Council of 1838 lowered this rating to 4s 2d per dollar, and another in 1843 tweaked the ratings in the Far East, but this was still not enough to bring more than a limited degree of monetary union to the British Empire.

British colonial territories from the 1820s onwards therefore found themselves in much the same position as American states, having in principle a common unit of account but remaining dependent on foreign coins for circulation. A few, such as Jamaica and Nova Scotia, issued a form of paper currency, and in British Guiana and the Cape of Good Hope, the imperial regime inherited from the Dutch an existing system of paper money, but most were suppressed in the 1830s.[61] The function of colonial banks in providing a circulating medium consequently attained an even greater importance in these colonies than in American states. This function, along with others, was thus subject to even closer and stricter regulation by the British imperial state than its federal counterpart exercised over state banks, frequently in parallel with efforts to regulate the note issue of British banks at home.[62] Between 1833 and 1846 a series of requirements were hammered out between the Treasury, the Board of Trade and the Colonial Office to restrict note issues to safe levels and prevent some of the problems observed in the more liberal regime of the United States. Banks were required to maintain a large specie reserve and redeem their notes in coin on demand, and colonies were forbidden from making their notes a legal tender. In practice these regulations were only intermittently observed until the 1850s, reflecting the uneven nature of British imperial authority, and the sheer size and scale of many of these banks meant that their notes thus obtained a very widespread circulation. This brought a useful degree of monetary unity to these regions, such as British North

America, British Australasia, the British Caribbean and British India, which was increasingly formalised in the late nineteenth century and helped underwrite the rise of sterling as the leading global currency after 1870.

Final Thoughts

In both the United States and the British Empire after 1783, politician and officials therefore continued to wrestle with the challenges created by diverse currencies and circulating media. Their strategies often closely resembled solutions first proposed between 1748 and 1768, reflecting the timelessness of the challenges and the processes by which they were addressed. Proposals continued to draw upon what writers considered to be best practice for currencies and banks, resulting in a promiscuous and often fairly uncritical and uninformed borrowing from American, English and Scottish examples. Yet these proposals were also shaped by broader ambitions, concerning the economic and political development of the British Atlantic and the commercial and imperial relationship between its various component parts. Monetary union was to achieve strategic consolidation, imperial centralisation and expansion of colonial economies and societies, sometimes simultaneously. They failed, even during the period between 1764 and 1767 when the British imperial state was arguably most open to ambitious and impractical colonial projects, since their elaborate plans for paper currencies were generally expensive, unwieldy and impractical, and in some cases the cure would have been worse than the disease. Only a sustained buy-in from imperial and colonial interests would have carried on these projects. And only when circumstances changed and monetary and financial union became a matter of national importance, as it did in the former British America between 1774 and 1787, did the political will exist to carry this forward.

Notes

1. See Chap. 1 and Edelson, *New map* p. 5.
2. Ibid. pp. 137–9, 241–7, 269–85.
3. Ibid. pp. 22–45, 197–287; D.H. Murdoch, 'Land policy in the eighteenth-century British empire: the sale of crown lands in the Ceded Islands, 1763–1783', *Historical Journal*, 27 (1984) pp. 549–74; Mark Quintanilla, 'Mercantile communities in the Ceded Islands: the Alexander Bartlet &

George Campbell Company', *International Social Science Review*, 79 (2004) pp. 14–26; Sheridan, *Sugar and slavery* pp. 452–9.
4. Edelson, *New map* pp. 155–9, 173–95.
5. Ernst, *Money and politics* pp. 104–5, 118.
6. See Chap. 1.
7. Ernst, *Money and politics* examines in detail the efforts for repeal (pp. 89–121) and the search for exemptions and loopholes (pp. 122–282, 312–49). See also Sosin, 'Imperial regulation', pp. 187–97; Greene and Jellison, 'Currency Act', pp. 489–514; Ferguson, *Power* pp. 20–3. The ministry proved willing, for instance, to allow New York to issue £100,000 in paper money after 1770 in order to support the quartering of imperial troops: Ernst, *Money and politics* pp. 264–81; Rabushka, *Taxation* pp. 797–9; P. D. G Thomas, *The Townshend duties crisis: the second phase of the American Revolution, 1767–1773* (Oxford, 1987) pp. 200–1.
8. Ernst, *Money and politics* pp. 282–311; Ferguson, *Power* p. 23; Sosin, 'Imperial regulation', pp. 197–8; Greene and Jellison, 'Currency Act', pp. 514–17.
9. For the Stamp Act, see Chap. 1. For the Sugar Act, see Sheridan, 'Molasses Act' pp. 62–83; O'Shaughnessy, *An empire divided* pp. 65–7; Allen S. Johnson, 'The passage of the Sugar Act', *William and Mary Quarterly*, 16 (1959) pp. 507–14; Rabushka, *Taxation* pp. 735–8, 752–4; Bullion, *Great and necessary measure* pp. 78–98.
10. See Chap. 1.
11. Ernst, *Money and politics* pp. 100–4.
12. See Chap. 1.
13. After all, both Stamp Act and Revenue Acts did collect some revenue: see Rabushka, *Taxation* pp. 751–8; O'Shaughnessy, *An empire divided* pp. 84–108; Barrow, *Trade and empire* pp. 244–8.
14. Bond, *Quit-rent system* pp. 505–6, 540, 542–3, 548–50, 640, 679–80, 688, 700–2, 845–6; Barrow, *Trade and empire* pp. 168–72, 188–208, 277–48; Alan D. Watson, 'The quitrent system in royal South Carolina', *William and Mary Quarterly*, 33 (1976) pp. 183–211.
15. Michener, 'Fixed exchange rates', pp. 250–3; Smith, 'American colonial monetary regimes', pp. 550–1; Michener, 'Redemption theories', pp. 321–4; Thayer, 'Land-Bank system', pp. 157–8.
16. Ernst, *Money and politics* pp. 153–65, 313–15.
17. See Chap. 3.
18. Niall Ferguson, 'Introduction. Virtual History: towards a "chaotic" theory of the past', in Niall Ferguson (ed.), *Virtual History: alternatives and counterfactuals* (London, 2003), quotation on p. 81; See also Jeremy Black, *Other pasts, different presents, alternative futures* (Bloomington, IN, 2015). For efforts to apply counterfactuals to the American Revolution, see

J.C.D. Clark, 'British America: what if there had been no American Revolution?', in Niall Ferguson (ed.), *Virtual History: alternatives and counterfactuals* (London, 2003) pp. 125–74; Black, *Other pasts* pp. 137–40; Robert February Sobel, *For want of a nail: if Burgoyne had won at Saratoga* (London, 1997); Jonathan Dull, *The miracle of American independence: twenty ways things could have turned out differently* (Lincoln, NE, 2015).
19. Horsefield, *Monetary experiments* pp. 125–35, 180–210, 244–7.
20. Graham, 'Corruption and contractors', pp. 1101–16; See also Ernst, *Money and politics* pp. 44–51.
21. TNA, WO34/98, f. 237r, Thomlinson, Hanbury, Colebrooke and Nesbitt to Hunter and Apthorp, 11 April 1759.
22. Graham, 'Corruption and contractors', pp. 1104–6; Brock, *Currency* pp. 345, 380–1; Rabushka, *Taxation* pp. 626–9; Ernst, *Money and politics* pp. 44–62.
23. TNA, WO34/197/2, p. 284, Amherst to Mortier, 30 May 1759.
24. BL, Add MS 32874 ff. 308r, 301r–312v, [Proposals].
25. See Chap. 3.
26. Horsefield, *Monetary experiments* pp. 129, 140–2. For abandoning interest on Bank of England notes, see Clapham, *Bank* vol. i, 22–3, 144.
27. Wright, *Origins* pp. 31–3; Ernst, *Money and politics* p. 95. For the prevailing rates of interest in private loans, see Roney, *Governed* pp. 107–8, 116, 118, 121–3, 127; Gwyn, *Enterprising admiral* pp. 95–6, 103, 105–7, 110–12, 117; Smith, *Slavery, family and gentry capitalism* pp. 147, 152, 154–5, 157, 168–9, 176; McCusker and Menard, *Economy of British America* p. 69n.
28. Graham, 'Corruption and contractors', p. 1114; David L. Preston, *Braddock's Defeat: the Battle of the Monongahela and the road to revolution* (Oxford, 2015) pp. 36–40, 76–7, 91–2, 106; Warren R. Hofstra, *The planting of New Virginia: settlement and landscape in the Shenandoah Valley* (Baltimore, MD, 2004) pp. 263–7.
29. Donald H. Kent and Sylvester Kirby Stevens (eds.), *The papers of Col. Henry Bouquet* (18 vols., Harrisburg, PA, 1940–1943) vol. vi, 56–7, Mercer to Bouquet, 28 August 1759.
30. See Chap. 3.
31. LBGA, A/12/4/D/105 #8965, 'Estimate of Profit and Loss on all the bills sold on account of the public', n.d. but circa 1791. This was, after all, nothing more than what the colonial governments were already doing on behalf of the imperial government and the British war effort.
32. Reed Browning, 'The Duke of Newcastle and the financing of the Seven Years' War', *Journal of Economic History*, 31 (1971) pp. 344–77; Stephen Conway, *War, state, and society in mid-eighteenth-century Britain and Ireland* (Oxford, 2006) pp. 83–114; Patrick O'Brien, 'The political

economy of British taxation, 1660–1815', *Economic History Review*, 2nd ser, 41 (1988) pp. 1–32.
33. See Chap. 1.
34. Ernst, *Money and politics* pp. 282–351. For the credit crisis of 1772, see Chap. 3. For mobilisation during the Falklands Crisis, see Geoffrey W. Rice, 'British foreign policy and the Falkland Islands crisis of 1770–1771', *International History Review*, 32 (2010) pp. 273–305; Nicholas Tracy, 'The Falkland Islands crisis of 1770; use of naval force', *English Historical Review*, 40 (1975) pp. 40–75. Instructions were sent to Gage in North America in 1770 to begin to expand regiments to their wartime size: see Shy, *Toward Lexington* p. 322.
35. For a survey, see Marshall, *Making and unmaking* pp. 273–310.
36. Greene and Jellison, 'Currency Act', pp. 516–18; Ernst, *Money and politics* pp. 317–18; Brock, *Currency* pp. 244–333; Rabushka, *Taxation* pp. 766–9.
37. Dickson, *Financial revolution* pp. 249–303; Wells and Willis, 'Revolution, restoration', pp. 418–41; Max M. Edling, *A Hercules in the cradle: war, money, and the American state, 1783–1867* (Oxford, 2014) pp. 84–8; Ferguson, *Power* pp. 140–71. Ferguson notes (p. 143) that 'the public debt was vital to the strategy of centralisation. As long as it belonged to Congress, it was a potential bond of union'.
38. Alexander Hamilton, 'The defence of the funding system' [July 1795] in Edling, *Hercules* p. 85.
39. CL, Germain Papers, vol. xvii (Undated Reports), No. 8, 'Insurrection—Paper Currency—Manifesto for Germans and Dutch—Vessels to be sunk in Philadelphia River' (undated but circa 1776–1777).
40. P. D. G Thomas, *Tea party to independence: the third phase of the American Revolution 1773–1776* (Oxford, 1991) pp. 143–75; Shy, *Toward Lexington* pp. 406–18; Bernard Donoughue, *British Politics and the American Revolution: the path to war, 1773–1775* (New York, 1964) pp. 177–230; Allan J. McCurry, 'The North Government and the outbreak of the American Revolution', *Huntington Library Quarterly*, 34 (1971) pp. 141–57; John Richard Alden, 'Why the march to Concord?', *American Historical Review*, 49 (1944) pp. 446–54.
41. CL, Gage Papers, English Correspondence, vol. xxvi, Gage to Dartmouth, 2 Sept. 1774, 30 Oct. 1774, and Gage to Barrington, 3 Oct. 1774.
42. CL, Gage Papers, English Correspondence, vol. xxvi, Dartmouth to Gage, 17 Oct. 1774, 27 Jan. 1775.
43. T. H. Breen, *American insurgents, American patriots: the revolution of the people* (New York, 2010) pp. 160–240; Richard D. Brown, *Revolutionary politics in Massachusetts: the Boston Committee of Correspondence and the towns, 1772–1774* (Cambridge, MA, 1970) pp. 178–236; David L. Ammerman, *In the common cause: American response to the Coercive acts*

of 1774 (Charlottesville, VA, 1974) pp. 73–124; Pauline Maier, *From resistance to revolution: colonial radicals and the development of American opposition to Britain, 1765–1776* (New York, 1972) pp. 241–53; Richard L. Bushman, *King and people in provincial Massachusetts* (Chapel Hill, NC, 1985) pp. 212–20.
44. CL, Gage Papers, English Correspondence, vol. xxvi, 2 Sept. 1774; Dartmouth to Gage, 17 Oct. 1774. For the Loyalist associations, see Thomas N. Ingersoll, *The Loyalist problem in revolutionary New England* (Cambridge, 2017) pp. 149–69; Maier, *Resistance to revolution* pp. 278–87.
45. Ferguson, *Power* p. 46.
46. Ronald Michener and Robert E. Wright, 'State "currencies" and the transition to the U.S. Dollar: clarifying some conclusions', *American Economic Review*, 95 (2005) pp. 683–7; Ferguson, *Power* pp. 26–69; Wright, *Origins* pp. 62–7; Edwin J. Perkins, *American public finance and financial services, 1700–1815* (Columbus, OH, 1994) pp. 85–105.
47. Bray Hammond, *Banks and politics in America: from the Revolution to the Civil War* (Princeton, NJ, 1957) pp. 40–53; Ferguson, *Power* pp. 122–40; Wright, *Origins* pp. 77–95; Perkins, *American public finance* pp. 106–36.
48. McCulloh, *Proposals for uniting the English colonies* pp. 24–5.
49. Edling, *Hercules* pp. 53–68; Michener and Wright, 'US monetary union', pp. 33–5; Michener and Wright, 'State "currencies"', pp. 687–92; Mary M. Schweitzer, 'State-issued currency and the ratification of the U.S. Constitution', *Journal of Economic History*, 49 (1989) pp. 311–22; Ferguson, *Power* pp. 179–250; Hammond, *Banks and politics* pp. 53–64, 89–113; Perkins, *American public finance* pp. 137–86.
50. Ferguson, *Power* p. 244.
51. Farley Grubb, 'Creating the U.S. dollar currency union 1748–1811; a quest for monetary stability or a usurpation of state sovereignty for personal gain?', *American Economic Review*, 93 (2003) pp. 1778–98; Schweitzer, 'State-issued currency', pp. 311–16; Ferguson, *Power* pp. 289–333; Michener and Wright, 'US monetary union', pp. 33–8; Michener and Wright, 'State "currencies"', esp. pp. 692–9; Hammond, *Banks and politics* pp. 89–113; Perkins, *American public finance* pp. 199–234.
52. Edling, *Hercules* pp. 17–49, 78–80, 224–46; Gautham Rao, 'The new historiography of the early Federal government: institutions, contexts and the imperial state', *William and Mary Quarterly*, 77 (2020) pp. 97–128; William J. Novak, 'The myth of the "weak" American state', *American Historical Review*, 113 (2008) pp. 752–72; Ferguson, *Power* pp. 289–305; Brian Balogh, *A government out of sight: the mystery of national authority in nineteenth-century America* (Cambridge, 2009) pp. 151–218.

53. Michener and Wright, 'US monetary union', p. 37. However, foreign coins made up most of the specie in circulation until the 1850s: David A. Martin, 'The changing role of foreign money in the United States, 1782–1857', *Journal of Economic History*, 37 (1977) pp. 1009–27.
54. This paragraph is based on Michener and Wright, 'US monetary union', pp. 37–40; Wright, *Origins* pp. 77–137; Hammond, *Banks and politics* pp. 114–630; Perkins, *American public finance* pp. 235–81; Howard Bodenhorn, *A history of banking in antebellum America: financial markets and economic development in an era of nation-building* (Cambridge and New York, 2000); Howard Bodenhorn, *State banking in early America: a new economic history* (Oxford and New York, 2003).
55. Edling, *Hercules* pp. 185–215; Hammond, *Banks and politics* pp. 671–739; Michener and Wright, 'US monetary union', p. 40.
56. Clapham, *Bank* vol. ii, 20–8, 21, 127; Desan, *Making money* pp. 311–20, 328; Wadan Narsey, *British Imperialism and the making of colonial currency systems* (London, 2016) pp. 23–32; Patrick O'Brien and Nuno Palma, 'Danger to the Old Lady of Threadneedle Street? The Bank Restriction Act and the regime shift to paper money, 1797–1821', *European Review of Economic History*, 24 (2020) pp. 390–426; Frank Whitson Fetter, *Development of British monetary orthodoxy, 1797–1875* (Fairfield, NJ, 1965), esp. pp. 59, 158–9.
57. Narsey, *British imperialism* pp. 55–6; Checkland, *Scottish banking* pp. 429–58; Munn, *Scottish provincial banking companies*; Saville, *Bank of Scotland* pp. 279–336; Barrow, *Emergence*; Philip Ollerenshaw, *Banking in nineteenth-century Ireland: the Belfast banks, 1825–1914* (Manchester, 1987) pp. 5–101. For the survival of the Pound Scots as a unit of account, see Fox, 'Monetary union of 1707', pp. 383–5.
58. Chalmers, *History of currency* pp. 23–32; Narsey, *British imperialism* pp. 58–67; W.H. Chaloner, 'Currency problems of the British Empire, 1814–1914', in B. M. Ratcliffe (ed.), *Great Britain and her world, 1750–1914: essays in honour of WO Henderson* (Manchester, 1975) pp. 179–202; H.A. Shannon, 'Evolution of the colonial sterling exchange standard', *Staff Papers (International Monetary Fund)*, 1 (1950–1951) pp. 334–41.
59. Chalmers, *History of currency* p. 417; See also Shannon, 'Colonial sterling exchange standard', pp. 350–4.
60. Chalmers, *History of currency* pp. 25–32 and passim; Chaloner, 'Currency problems', pp. 179–202; Narsey, *British imperialism* pp. 58–64; Shannon, 'Colonial sterling exchange standard', pp. 341–4.
61. E. H. D. Arndt, *Banking and currency development in South Africa: 1652–1927* (Cape Town, 1928) pp. 5–69; Chalmers, *History of currency*

pp. 109–12, 124–35, 189–90, 230–6; McCullough, *Money and exchange in Canada* pp. 139–42, 151–3.
62. Shannon, 'Colonial sterling exchange standard', pp. 344–5; Chalmers, *History of currency* pp. 32–7 and *passim*; Jones, *British multinational banking* pp. 19–20, 108–9; Baster, *The imperial banks* pp. 20–48. For British regulation, see P. L. Cottrell, '"Conservative abroad, liberal at home": British banking regulation during the nineteenth century', in Jaime Reis and Stefano Battilossi (eds.), *State and financial systems in Europe and the USA: historical perspectives on regulation and supervision in the nineteenth and twentieth centuries* (Farnham, 2016) pp. 21–39; John H. Wood, *A history of central banking in Great Britain and the United States* (Cambridge, 2005) pp. 32–116. For US regulation, see Perkins, *American public finance* pp. 32–44; Jill M. Hendrickson, *Regulation and instability in U.S. commercial banking: a history of crises* (Basingstoke and New York, 2011) pp. 24–73; Wood, *History* pp. 117–52.

Appendix A: Sir Alexander Cuming, Commonplace Book (Circa 1764 to 1767)

Newberry Library, Chicago, Illinois
 Ayer MS 204

Since a National Bank formed on right principles has been evidently distinguished by the wisdom of Providence as the true Philosopher's Stone in a well governed state, as preferable by far to the richest mines of gold and silver for promoting an honest industry and for increasing the power and wealth of such a state, I humbly conceived my duty called upon me to suggest to your wisdom and virtues the principle of such a Bank

1st for improving the British colonies in America and elsewhere
2nd for preserving them at the same time in a natural and easy state of dependency on Great Britain, their Mother Country.
3rd for paying the national debts of Great Britain
4th for acquiring a gain of 200 millions of pounds sterling in gold and silver specie in 40 years as the fruits of an honest industry
5th to be enabled thereby to lend unto many nations without borrowing.
6th to civilise the Indian and American savages etc. so as to induce them to become faithful subjects to the Crown of Great Britain.
7th that the wisdom of His Majesty's councils might be enabled by such principles to execute the principles recommended by infinite wisdom for the general benefit of mankind as true and faithful servants of that mighty Being by whom we all exist.

I humbly conceive that credit for one million of pounds sterling only would be sufficient to attain the several ends here suggested in less than half a century if rightly directed and managed by wise and upright men upon true Patriotick Principles for the real interest of these kingdoms and for the general benefit of mankind as servants of our righteous Lord under the government of King George the Third.

The Principles here suggest are as follows, vizt

1st, that all the public taxes ought to be made payable in notes formed by the wisdom of the state for that purpose.
2nd, that there should be a Bank of a certain number of ounces of standard silver coined or not coined into which the bearers of such notes may be entitled to realise the said notes at the Bank on demand. And that there should be also a certain number of ounces of standard gold coined or not coined into which the bearers of notes expressing the value thereof in gold may be enabled to realise the said notes into gold, at the Bank, on demand
3rd, that the notes may be lent out to the several members of the community upon good and sufficient security for the conveniency of circulation and for promoting useful knowledge, arts and an honest industry, and for increasing the power and wealth of such a well governed state.
4th, that the borrowers of such notes should be obliged to pay interest for the same at certain stated times appointed by the wisdom of the state for that purpose.
5th, that the gain arising from the said interest should be realised from time to time into a certain number of ounces of standard silver and standard gold.
6th, that four millions of ounces of standard silver, after the abovementioned regulations take place, will soon be able to circulate notes to the value of twelve millions of ounces of such standard silver, and will enable the Bank at the same time to pay all the above-mentioned Bank notes on demand to such as can be enabled to make a demand for the said silver. Hence an interest of fifteen per cent may be made by the Bank when each borrower is only obliged to pay five per cent per annum for the sums he shall happen to borrow.
7th, one million pounds sterling may be doubled in five years when so managed as to produce a real gain of fifteen percent per annum, and that gain accumulated for five years.

8th, and by the same way of reasoning the amount of the said Bank may be grossly represented by the following scheme, vizt

Years	Millions
5	£2
10	£4
15	£8
20	£16
25	£32
30	£64
35	£128
40	£256

So that from a credit originally given by the wisdom of the state for only one million of pounds sterling a gain might be made from thence of 200 millions of pounds sterling, besides 55 millions for the charges of management, and the one million credited might be returned at the expiration of forty years.

The principles of a National Bank suggested here are these, vizt

1st, that the wisdom and honour of the state as residing in the Legislature ought to be the source of credit given to all the particular members of the state, supposing the several members that constitute the Legislature to be both wise and honest.
2nd, that this credit should be lent to the several members of the community who have occasion for credit as the means to promote an honest industry and to execute any well concerted plan for public benefit.
3rd, that the borrowers of this credit should be obliged to pay interest for the credit given, on account of its enabling them to acquire a gain to themselves many times the value of the interest they contract to pay for the said credit.
4th, the gain here suggested will arise from the credit given to the borrowers to the knowledge, ingenuity, arts, industry and honesty of the borrowers, and to the right use they are enabled to make of the said credit by the wisdom and honour of the state.

The interest thus paid by the borrowers under the direction of the wise state and upright administration would be sufficient to produce a revenue of six millions sterling per annum in less than half a century. And a Bank of one million of pounds sterling laid aside for this purpose would be sufficient to supply the borrowers with as much gold and silver specie as could be requisite for circulating Bank credit for half a century to the value of two hundred and sixty millions of pounds sterling.

The truth of these Principles is capable of being demonstrated by a plain and obvious matter of fact.

Appendix B: Lauchlin Macleane to the Earl of Hertford 'Proposal' (1765)

William L. Clements Library, Ann Arbor, Michigan
Shelburne Papers, Volume 49 No. 50

Several incidents concurred at the conclusion of the last war, and still continue to distress the inhabitants of North America in respect of their commerce and credit.

During the war the demand of European commodities was very great, especially for the manufactures of England. I might venture to say double of what was usual in times of peace. This increase in demands was occasioned principally by three causes,

1st, the large army employed on the Continent
2nd, the fleets sent thither from time to time.
3rd, the supplies required by our enemies whose Communication with Europe was entirely cut off during the last years of the war, hence arose what was vulgarly called the Flag of Truce trade.

An increase of credit to the buyers is the natural consequence of an increase of trade, of course therefore the merchants of North America become deeply indebted to the merchants of Great Britain and as the precise period of the Peace could not be foreseen by the adventures in Commerce, a larger stock of European goods must necessarily remain on the hands of the merchants whenever a Peace should take place than would be sufficient for the subsequent sales. Therefore it was natural to expect that upon the conclusion of a Peace credit must receive a severe shock, for the demand for British commodities ceasing all at once, the English merchants would naturally become anxious for their outstanding debts, compulsive methods to obtain payment would be [?recurred] to, and consequently many bankruptcies would ensue.

This in fact was the case, and therefore the first years of a Peace would seem very improper season to introduce violent innovations, to lay on new taxes, and to abolish paper credit. Could this fail to increase the confusion, to raise a spirit of clamours and discontent, and to occasion an opposition to measures which otherwise would have been thought highly reasonable and which would not have met with the smallest obstruction at a more seasonable opportunity.

Though the Provinces of North America are greatly in debt to England, yet they are a thriving and happy people, and very able to pay much heavier taxes than are imposed upon them, for the debts of North America bear no proportion to the National Debt of England, great part of which has been contracted in support of the Colonies. The *time* therefore and perhaps the *mode* of imposing the tax in question are the only circumstances which can admit of complaint while the tax itself is not only equitable but necessary.

On the other hand it ought to be considered that most part of the internal debt of North America outstanding bills of credit has been contracted in support of the war, that these bills are to be sunk by duties voluntarily imposed by themselves upon their commerce, and therefore that every restraint thrown upon their commerce and every measure tending to affect the credit of their bills prior to the periods allotted for their being called in may be thought severe and premature.

Should the Funds destined for the discharge of the current paper be insufficient to sink it within their limited time while the tender of the said paper is declared not to be legal after the expiration of that time, it is easier to foresee the confusion and distress of the different Provinces than to remedy them. The Provinces alone of Virginia, Maryland, Pennsylvania, New Jersey and New York cannot have bills of credit outstanding at present to little less amount than one million sterling.

Yet it must be confessed that great abuses arose from the unrestrained profusion with which some of the Provinces issued their paper money without attending to any rational method of forming funds for calling in the same, insomuch that the bills issued in several of the Northern

Provinces had depreciated below a tenth part of their original value and these Provinces were therefore very deservedly restrained in this particular by Act of Parliament in the Reign of His late Majesty.

This however was not the case in all the Provinces for though the bills of North Carolina have long and those of Virginia have lately fallen into disrepute, yet the bills emitted in New York, New Jersey, Pennsylvania and South Carolina never depreciated, and in Maryland where they were lately made to bear interest they have gained in value so as to bear a premium.

Hence it appears that the error did not lie in issuing bills of credit, but in not providing adequate funds for sinking the same, for it cannot be said that the sums issued in any of the Provinces were sufficient to affect the intrinsic value of cash. Nay, on the contrary, it may be demonstrated that in a Country much in debt, and daily wanting cash for remittance, there is an absolutely necessity for such a quantity of paper credit as will serve for a medium of commerce, without diminishing the intrinsic value of the current species. And such paper currency is in reality more valuable in one respect than cash, for being of no intrinsic worth for remittances, it must remain in the Provinces to answer the purposes of trade while the current coin may from time to time be remitted to England without detriment to commerce.

It would therefore seem highly deserving the attention of Government to take proper measures for preventing the Calamities which threaten the Provinces from the entire abolition of their paper currency, and the remedy is easy and very natural; it is only taking into the hands of Government that power which the Provinces have ever been too apt to abuse. A Loan Office established in each Province by Act of Parliament would remove entirely all case of complaint and re-establish credit, give new life and vigour to a declining Commerce, and thereby enable the Colonies to pay their debts to the Mother Country. A point in which the merchants of London, who are the principal creditors, are no less interested than the Colonies themselves.

A measure which is at the same time calculated for the advantage of Individuals and for the service of the state cannot well fail of being popular, and this measure includes both, for while £80,000 sterling clear of all deductions may be paid into the Exchequer annually from the interest, the private merchant will be enabled to trade upon the credit of his lands and of his chattels, as often as his cash shall happen by remittances or otherwise to be exhausted.

The Provinces of North America are indebted to Great Britain by the best calculations about three million sterling, a constant circulation therefore of one million and a half in paper would enable the Colonies to remit one half of their debt upon the credit of their lands and it is a question not easily to be determined I believe whether it would be for the interest of the mother Country that her Colonies were much less indebted to her.

In order to prevent all the bills from being collected to the provinces of most extensive trade which in some measure would defeat the intention of the Government, it would seem eligible that the Provinces should each have their respective Quotas of the Loan, in their respective Currencies. The Exchange of each to be regulated by the intrinsic value of the Spanish milled dollar which is the prevailing coin of the Colonies.

The following Scheme is formed on the foregoing principles. It is not offered as prefect, but only as an elucidation of what has been advanced.

Canada	£100,000	
Nova Scotia	£50,000	£150,000
New Hampshire	£60,000	
Massachusetts	£150,000	
Connecticut	£50,000	
Rhode Island	£50,000	
New York	£150,000	
Jerseys	£70,000	
Pennsylvania	£150,000	
Maryland	£100,000	
Virginia	£150,000	
N Carolina	£70,000	
S Carolina	£130,000	
Georgia	£40,000	
E Florida	£40,000	
W Florida	£30,000	£1,440,000
Jamaica	£150,000	
Grenada	£60,000	
Tobago	£30,000	
St Vincent	£50,000	
Dominica	£50,000	
Antigua	£50,000	
St Kitts	£50,000	
Montserrat	£30,000	
Nevis	£20,000	
Barbados	£100,000	£410,000
Total:		£2,000,000

Interest of money in America may be taken at an average of 6 pct. Therefore the amount of 6 percent on two millions annual is £120,000

Deduct charges say 2 percent	£40,000
Neat profit to the Treasury in case entire Loan circulated	£80,000

To keep the entire Loan in circulation the Cashier of each Office should have discretionary power to issue notes on emergency to a certain amount above the regular proportion allowed for each Province.

Officers Requisite
    3 Receiver Generals vizt
        1 for S District of America
        1 for N District of America
        1 for the Islands
    For each Loan Office,
        Cashier
        Two clerks
        Solicitor to draw Deeds
        Appraiser
        Chamber keeper
        Porter

The Principal Officers to give sufficient security.

Appendix C: Charles Williamos 'Plan for Establishing a Bank in North America' (c. 1766)

Staffordshire Record Office, Stafford, Staffordshire
Dartmouth Papers, D(W) 1778/II/762
Prohibition of Paper currency in N[orth] A[merica]'s effect tho' it has not taken place yet

Tho the Prohibition of Paper Currency in the several provinces of North America, has as yet taken place in few or none intirely, as the time their Bills have to run is not expired, it has notwithstanding caused great distress, and inconveniency already as many of the Notes were fixed by the Assemblies to be called in by a certain time in some already elapsed and that they have not Liberty by the late Act of Parliament to Issue new ones till it takes place.

Inhabitants not able to send for goods from Britain, and hardly likely to live at home

The Northern Colonies having no established staple suffer most, having no means by their returns of the produce of their Country, to pay for the many things they want from Great Britain, and hardly to have wherewithal to supply themselves with the most common necessaries of Life, whereby many Inhabitants or Planters whose Estates are worth some thousands of Pounds are obliged to deprive themselves of almost everything for Want of the most trifling Sums to go to market, as there is so little bullion in the whole Continent that one might Travell for many Miles without finding any Coin whatsoever

This is a great stop to trade

from which must necessarily derive a very great stop in the Trade,

Prevents settling and improving the lands

the Settling or Emproving the Colonies, as they have not or cannot procure the most necessary Article to carry either into Execution much less to any degree of perfection.

Must be severely felt at home after Act takes place

A very short time must augment or indeed compleat their distress as their present Paper Bills are soon to be intirely at an End, and they must be drove thereby to the necessity of confining themselves to the produce of their Estates only: which must be sensibly felt by all our Manufacturers at home as the Colonists will not be able to purchase their goods, unless the Legislature falls upon some method of making up the Loss incurred by the suppression of their own paper currency by finding some means to answer the same purpose.

Mother Country considered

The advantage of the Mother Country, should at the same time be duly consider'd,

Revenue improved by it

the revenue improved by it to take off from the heavy Taxes the subjects of Great Britain are obliged to pay,

Dependency of the colonies on mother country secured

and the dependency of the Colonies on the Mother Country secured, which can no ways be so effectually done as by making their own Interest and that of Great Britain coincide in all things if possible,

By taking them from manufacturing for themselves

by taking them of, from Manufacturing for themselves, and bringing as far as practicable the nature of their Estates to depend on Great Britain.

Method proposed

Many are (it must be supposed) the Plans laid before the Government for that purpose

Establish[in]g an American Bank

but one of the most advantageous would be that of Establishing an American Bank on the Plan following.
　The Assemblies of the different colonies should first make an estimate as accurate and as explicit as possible of the value of the Lands in their respective provinces.

Lands to be valued every 5 years by assemblies

This Estimate after being approved of by the Governor and Council to be Printed for the Use of the Bank, mentioning particularly the Counties, Rivers, Low, High, good and bad Lands of each with their real Value, which Estimate shou'd be renewed or alter'd every five years as the Worth of the lands in America increases much in a short time.

General Bank with notes in sterling or other of different value

A General Bank for America should then be Established by the Government at home with notes of different value in sterling or other currency, which should be done on the same Paper and after the manner of the Bank Notes of England to prevent their being counterfeited,

Notes to be current throughout whole Continent

these Notes should then be made by Act of Parliament, current through the whole Continent, and even at home (if found practical) for the payment of all Debts whatsoever;

Issued to colonies at rate of £10 per man

some Millions to be issued for the whole and distributed to the different Colonies at the rate of ten Pounds more or less for every free Man possessed of Lands in the provinces; and as it would be very inconvenient to have Notes for trifling sums wanted, a certain quantity of small silver or other coin should be made part of the whole Bank, which coin should either be raised twenty-five Per Cent above its real value or depreciated of the same in the Alloy to prevent its being carried out of the Country.

Lords of the Treasury to issue notes to different colonies, appoint distributors and have the supreme direction

The Lords Commissioners of the Treasury to have supreme direction of the Bank, to issue at first to the different colonies their proportion of notes and coin, and appoint a distributor in each.

A Court of directors should be appointed besides for North America to be held at New York and meet there once a year, of which the Governor of said Province the Commander in Chief of his Majestys forces or other great Officers that the Lords of the Treasury should appoint ought to be Members.

Court of Directors established to meet yearly in New York

This Court of Directors to be besides composed of Members sent (one by each) by the Colonies

Elected by each province by stockholder of £100 and upwards

and Elected by the Majority in each province of those possessed of £100 or upwards of Bank Notes upon their Bonds; these Directors to be reelected once in five Years and the Court to choose a chairman.

The Distributors of each province after the Establishing of the Court of Directors should be under the inspection of that Court, as well

Distributors of each province after establishment of Bank to be under the inspection of the Court, and all matters relating to said General Bank,

To have sole direction of all matters relative to Bank under Lords of the Treasury

to whom after first exportation the Treasury should send any further supply of notes as might be wanted

To take security from Distributors

and who should also take sufficient security from Distributors.

Bank Notes of each colony to be under care of Governor and Council and issued by them to the Distributors

The Governor and Council of each province should have under their care the Sums allotted for it and to issue any part of it to the Distributors tho' not more than £20,000 at a time and Directors Elected in the province for time being to have a seat in Council.

Every landholder entitled to take cash from the Bank upon producing his title certified by the Surveyor-General and Receiver of Quit Rents upon mortgaging the said lands or any part of them by his bond upon paying interest for said cash.
Bond to be redeemed on paying sum borrowed with interest.

Every man in each Province possessed of Lands should be intitled to take up Bank Notes from Distributor upon producing his Titles to said Lands certified by Surveyor general and Receiver-General of the Quit Rents, and on Mortgaging said Lands or any part of them by a Bond ready for that purpose at the Distributor's Office, and the condition of said Bond to be an Interest of not less than two Per Cent nor more than three and a half for the money taken upon the said Bond, which at any time might be redeemed on repaying the sum borrowed with the Interest due.

Distributors made answerable not to give more than half the value of the lands according to the Estimate in their hands

The Distributors to prevent frauds to the Government should be very careful and made Answerable not to give more than half of value of Lands on the Mortgaging Bonds according to the Estimate in their Hands established by the Assemblies for that purpose.

Bonds to be paid for by mortgagees at rate of 1 Per Cent

The Bonds to be paid for by Person taking up money at rate of 1 Per Cent to defray the expences attending the Establishment of the Bank.

Distributors Accounts to be inspected once a month by Directors of every province, and yearly by the Court of Directors and sent by them in General Return to Treasury

The Distributors should be supplied with more money by the Governors and Councils upon producing their accounts certified by the Director of the Province they belong to, that they have disposed of and received Bonds for all the Cash they had in their Hands, exclusive of which the Distributors

Account should be inspected every Month by the Directors and afterwards sent yearly and strictly looked into by Court of Directors at New York; who should at close of their settling transmit to the Lords Commissioners of the Treasury an Exact and General return of sums taken up, Names of the People, situation of Lands Mortgaged, and sums repaid in Respective provinces.

Appointment of Directors and other Officers of the Bank.

Directors might have for their appointment £1,000 Per Annum, the Distributors 5 Per Cent on the Interest received by them, The Secretary to the Court of Directors £500 Per Annum for himself and Clerks and the Receiver General appointed to collect the Yearly Revenue from the different distributors, and to Issue any further sus to the Provinces as applied to by them and approved of by the Court of Directors should have 1 Per Cent upon the revenue collected and what should remain afterwards be employed towards the maintaining of the Troops or other necessary Expences of the Government.

This Plan proposed to the provinces

This Proposed Plan appears the most eligible from the easy Method of putting it into Execution from the considerable revenue it would bring to the Crown,

Most agreeable to the Americans

but much more so by the great advantages, that would accrue from thence to the Continent of North America to the inhabitants, of which it would be very agreeable as all those to whom it has already been proposed (which are almost the greatest in number and wealth of four of the most considerable colonies vizt South and North Carolina, Virginia & Maryland in a journey very lately undertook through these Provinces) all wished such Plan might take place

Because every man could get money on his own landed security

because by that means every man could get money upon his own Landed Security without any Collateral one;

Because would take them out of the hands of money-lenders who exact in some provinces 8 Per Cent

because it would take them out of the hands of Money Lenders, who distress them very much by their securities and high Interest, not less in some Provinces than 8 Per Cent and that every Estate in America would easily produce more than sufficient to pay a small Interest

Because they might easily get money to improve their estates

and principally because they might without difficulty get cash to improve their estates which now lay mostly useless as all the Planters in general cannot even procure enough to bring up and subsist their Families and much less make upon their Lands the improvement they could wish,

The produce of which would centre in England

which would at the end center in Great Britain as the high price of labour in the Colonies does not permit the inhabitants to manufacture for themselves within Fifty Per Cent of what they can get their goods from Great Britain.

Estimate
An Estimate of the whole Plan

A Million of People, each to take £10	£10,000,000
Interest of 10 Million @ 3 Per Cent	£300,000
Expenses to be Deducted	£33,500
Revenue to Govt by Balance	£266,500
15 Directors @ £1,000 Per Annum	£15,000
15 Distributors @ 5 Per Cent for £300,000	£15,000
Receiver General @ 1 Per Cent for D[itt]o	£3,000
Secretary to the Court of Directors	£500
Total:	£33,500

Appendix D: 'Proposals for Establishing Paper Currency in North America' (Undated but c. 1767)[1]

William L. Clements Library, Ann Arbor, Michigan
Charles Townshend Papers, Box 8 Folder 39/5

That a patent joint-stock company be established in London, to be called the Company of Merchants trading in Exchanges with the Colonies or any other title that shall be thought most proper.

That the Capital Stock of the said Company shall amount to £100,000 sterling to be raised by voluntary subscriptions of merchants and others that chose to be proprietors.

That the Parliament be petitioned to establish the same Company by charter.

That a Court of Directors shall be annually chosen by the proprietors.

That £1,000 stock shall be a qualification for a Director, and £500 stock shall be a qualification for a proprietor to vote at all General Courts.

That there shall be a Chamber of Management in each of the Colonies where it shall be thought necessary, each Chamber consisting of [blank] Members with salaries and allowance for clerks and other charges.

That £1,000 of Stock shall qualify a person to be a member of a Chamber of Directions in the Colonies.

That the Members of the Chambers of Direction shall be named by the Court of Directors in London, and subject to their Orders.

That it shall be lawful for the Court of Directors to order their Chamber of Management in the Colonies to issue out bills or notes for carrying on the currency of North America in any sums not less than five shillings sterling, and also to draw bills of exchange of larger sums at [blank] days sight on the Court of Directors in London.

That it is humbly proposed that the small notes or bills for supplying the Currency of the Colonies shall be in the following form

£1 sterling	Boston 1 January 1768

The Chamber of Boston promise to account to Mr A.B. or Bearer for one pound sterling in January 1769 value received by Order of the Court of Directors.

A.B.	C.D.

NB: In the Option of the Holders this note will be paid in London after fifteen months by the Cashier to the Company of Merchants trading in Exchange with the Colonies

That the said Chambers shall always issue their said notes at 365 days date, and bills of exchange at three months sight, to all who shall tender them silver at the rate of $5¼$d sterling per oz and gold at the rate of £4 per ounce for the same.

That the said Chambers shall also liquidate any sum of their notes that are become payable, and are demanded not less than £50 to one person at one time, or in one bill.

That the Court of Directors may instruct the said Chambers to draw bills on one another, and thereby establish a Course of Exchange in the Colonies.

That the directors of the Company in London shall also draw bills on the Colonies if required.

That the Currency of all the Colonies shall be sterling money or notes.

That to enable the Chambers of the Colonies to make remittances to England for retiring their bills of exchange and notes, they shall be at liberty to purchase and remit and ship to Great Britain only any of the enumerated goods of the said Colonies.

That it shall be lawful for the said Company to discount bills or notes of hand, lend money on bonds, mortgages or other securities they shall think proper in the said Colonies, at an interest of 6 pct per annum, also that they may open cash accounts with any person or persons in the said

Colonies for certain sums upon sufficient security, all advances on said accounts to bear the above interest, and all moneys paid to be in the Company's notes.

That on obtaining from Government an exclusive charter and privilege to the above effect for years they shall pay to Government Ten Thousand pounds per annum.

That each of the following Colonies shall choose a Director in London, provided the Members chose[n] by the Colonies are not more than one third of the whole number, and that each of them be possessed of £ Capital Stock.

Note

1. The document is undated but it seems plausible to date it to 1767 because the model bill of exchange provided as a template in the 'Proposals' is dated 1 January 1768.

Bibliography

Manuscript Sources

British Library

Add. Ms. 11514
Add. Ms. 30163
Add. Ms. 32714
Add. Ms. 32874
Add. Ms. 39855
RP 380/2 Reel 2

Clements Library

Charles Townshend Papers, Box 8, Folder 39/5
Germain Papers, vol. xvii no. 8
Gage Papers, English Correspondence, vol. xxvi
Shelburne Papers, vol. 49 no. 50

Huntington Library

STG Box 12 No. 28

Lloyds Banking Group Archives

A/12/4/D/105, #8965

NEWBERRY LIBRARY
Ayer MS, MS 204

JOHN RYLANDS LIBRARY
Egerton of Tatton MS, EGT/2/6/2/66

STAFFORDSHIRE RECORD OFFICE
Dartmouth MS, DW 1778/ii/218
Dartmouth MS, DW 1778/ii/762

THE NATIONAL ARCHIVES OF THE UNITED KINGDOM
CO 5/361
CO 323/12
PRO 30/8/97
SP 36/19/1
T1/371/62
WO 34/98
WO 34/197

PRINTED SOURCES

Boston Daily News-Letter no. 187 (23 to 30 July 1730)
Cuming, Sir Alexander, *The case of Sir Alexander Cuming Bart, truly stated, in relation to merchants in So[uth] Carolina* (London, 1730)
Colonial and State Records of North Carolina (26 vols, 1886–1907, Winston, NC)
The Grenville Papers: being the correspondence of Richard Grenville ... [and] George Grenville ed. William James Smith (4 vols, London 1852-3)
The Journal of the Commons House of Assembly of South Carolina ed. J.H. Easterby et al. (14 vols, Columbia, SC, 1951–89)
Letters and papers of Benjamin Franklin and Richard Jackson, 1753–1785 ed. Carl van Doren (Philadelphia, PA, 1947)
Lysons, Daniel, *The environs of London, being an historical account of the towns, villages, and hamlets, within twelve miles of that capital, interspersed with biographical anecdotes* (2 vols., London, 1811)
McCulloh, Henry, *Proposals for uniting the English colonies on the continent of America, so as to enable them to act with force and vigour against their enemies* (London, 1757)
———, *Miscellaneous representations relative to our Concerns in America, submitted in 1761–to the Earl of Bute* (London, 1905 [1761])

The papers of Col. Henry Bouquet, ed. Donald H. Kent and Sylvester Kirby Stevens (18 vols, Harrisburg, PA, 1940–3)
Statutes at Large of Pennsylvania from 1682–1801 ed. James T. Mitchell and Henry Flanders (14 vols, Harrisburg, PA, 1896–1909)
Pownall, Thomas, *The administration of the colonies: wherein their rights and constitution are discussed and stated* (London, 1768)

SECONDARY SOURCES

Ackrill, Margaret and Hannah, Leslie, *Barclays: the business of banking, 1690–1996* (Cambridge: Cambridge University Press, 2001)
Alden, John Richard, 'Why the march to Concord?', *American Historical Review*, 49 (1944) pp. 446–54
Ammerman, David L., *In the common cause: American response to the Coercive acts of 1774* (Charlottesville, VA: University Press of Virginia, 1974)
Anderson, B. L., 'Money and the structure of credit in the 18th century', *Business History*, 12 (1970) pp. 85–101
Andreas, Peter, *Smuggler nation: how illicit trade made America* (New York: Oxford University Press, 2013)
Armitage, David, *The ideological origins of the British Empire* (Cambridge: Cambridge University Press, 2000)
Armytage, Frances, *The free port system in the British West Indies: a study in commercial policy, 1766–1822* (London: Royal Empire Society by Longmans, Green & Co., 1953)
Arndt, E. H. D., *Banking and currency development in South Africa: 1652–1927* (Cape Town: Juta & Co., 1928)
Baker, Norman, *Government and contractors: the British Treasury and war supplies, 1775–1783* (London: Athlone Press, 1971)
Balogh, Brian, *A government out of sight: the mystery of national authority in nineteenth-century America* (Cambridge: Cambridge University Press, 2009)
Bargar, B. D., *Lord Dartmouth and the American Revolution* (Columbia, SC: University of South Carolina Press, 1965)
Barnwell, Joseph W., 'Garth Correspondence (continued)', *South Carolina Historical and Genealogical Magazine*, 29 (1928) pp. 212–30
Barrow, Lennox, *The emergence of the Irish banking system, 1820–1845* (Dublin: Gill and Macmillan, 1975)
Barrow, Thomas C., *Trade and empire: the British customs service in colonial America 1660–1775* (Cambridge, MA: Harvard University Press, 1967)
Barth, Jonathan Edward, '"A peculiar stampe of our owne": the Massachusetts Mint and the battle over sovereignty, 1652–1691', *New England Quarterly*, 87 (2014) pp. 490–525
Baster, A.S.J., *The imperial banks* (London: P.S. King, 1929)

Billias, George Athan, *The Massachusetts land bankers of 1740* (Orono, ME: The University Press, 1959)
Binney, J.E.D., *British public finance and administration, 1774–92* (Oxford: Clarendon Press, 1958)
Black, Iain S., 'Private banking in London's West End, 1750–1830', *London Journal*, 28 (2003) pp. 29–59
Black, Jeremy, *Other pasts, different presents, alternative futures* (Bloomington, IN: Indiana University Press, 2015)
Bodenhorn, Howard, *A history of banking in antebellum America: financial markets and economic development in an era of nation-building* (Cambridge and New York: Cambridge University Press, 2000)
———, *State banking in early America: a new economic history* (Oxford and New York: Oxford University Press, 2003)
Bond, Beverley W., *The quit-rent system in the American colonies* (New Haven: Yale University Press, 1919)
Bowen, H. V., 'Lord Clive and speculation in East India Company stock, 1766', *Historical Journal*, 30 (1987) pp. 905–20
Bowler, R. Arthur, *Logistics and the failure of the British Army in America, 1775–1783* (Princeton, NJ: Princeton University Press, 1975)
Breen, T. H., *American insurgents, American patriots: the revolution of the people* (New York: Farrar, Straus and Giroux, 2010)
Brock, Leslie V., *The currency of the American colonies, 1700–1764: a study in colonial finance and imperial relations* (New York: Arno Press, 1975)
Brooke, John L., *The heart of the Commonwealth: society and political culture in Worcester County, Massachusetts, 1713–1861* (Cambridge: Cambridge University Press, 1989)
Brown, Richard D., *Revolutionary politics in Massachusetts: the Boston Committee of Correspondence and the towns, 1772–1774* (Cambridge, MA: Harvard University Press, 1970)
Browning, Reed, 'The Duke of Newcastle and the financing of the Seven Years' War', *Journal of Economic History*, 31 (1971) pp. 344–77
Bullion, John L., *A great and necessary measure: George Granville and the genesis of the Stamp Act 1763–1765* (Columbia, MO: University of Missouri Press, 1982)
———., '"The ten thousand in America": more light on the decision on the American army, 1762–1763', *William and Mary Quarterly*, 43 (1986) pp. 646–57
Bumsted, J.M., '"Things in the womb of time": ideas of American Independence, 1633 to 1763', *William and Mary Quarterly*, 31 (1974) pp. 533–64
———., 'A forgotten prophet: Henry McCulloh and reform of the British Empire', *Canadian Review of American Studies*, 13 (1982) pp. 1–14
Bushman, Richard L., *King and people in provincial Massachusetts* (Chapel Hill, NC: Published for the Institute of Early American History and Culture, Williamsburg, VA, by the University of North Carolina Press, 1985)

Caffentzis, Constantine, 'Why did Berkeley's bank fail? Money and libertinism in eighteenth-century Ireland', *Eighteenth-century Ireland/Iris an dá chultúr*, 12 (1997) pp. 100–15

Cannon, John, 'Petty [*formerly* Fitzmaurice], William, second earl of Shelburne and first marquess of Lansdown (1737–1805)', *ODNB* [https://doi.org/10.1093/ref:odnb/22070, accessed 23 Feb. 2020]

Carey, Daniel and Finlay, Christopher (eds.), *The empire of credit: the financial revolution in the British Atlantic world, 1688–1815* (Dublin: Irish Academic Press, 2011)

Carter, Clarence Edwin, *Great Britain and the Illinois country, 1763–1774* (Washington, DC: American Historical Association, 1910)

Chalmers, Robert, *A history of currency in the British colonies* (London: Eyre & Spottiswoode, 1893)

Chaloner, W.H., 'Currency problems of the British Empire, 1814–1914', in B. M. Ratcliffe (ed.), *Great Britain and her world, 1750–1914: essays in honour of WO Henderson* (Manchester: Manchester University Press, 1975) pp. 153–78

Chandaman, C.D., *The English public revenue, 1660–1688* (Oxford: Oxford University Press, 1975)

Checkland, S. G., *Scottish banking: a history, 1695–1973* (Glasgow: Collins, 1975)

Clapham, J. H., *The Bank of England: a history* (Cambridge: Cambridge University Press, 1945)

Clark, Dora Mae, 'The British Treasury and the administration of military affairs in America, 1754–1774', *Pennsylvania History*, 2 (1935) pp. 197–204

———, 'The American Board of Customs, 1767–1783', *American Historical Review*, 45 (1940) pp. 777–806

Clark, J.C.D., 'British America: what if there had been no American Revolution?', in Niall Ferguson (ed.), *Virtual History: alternatives and counterfactuals* (London: Pan, 2003) pp. 125–74

Conway, Stephen, *War, state, and society in mid-eighteenth-century Britain and Ireland* (Oxford: Oxford University Press, 2006)

Cope, S.R., 'The Goldsmids and the development of the London money market during the Napoleonic Wars', *Economica*, 9 (1942) pp. 180–206

Cottrell, P. L., '"Conservative abroad, liberal at home": British banking regulation during the nineteenth century', in Jaime Reis and Stefano Battilossi (eds.), *State and financial systems in Europe and the USA: historical perspectives on regulation and supervision in the nineteenth and twentieth centuries* (Farnham: Ashgate, 2016) pp. 21–40

Courtney, W.P. and Alter, J.M., 'Jackson, Richard, (1721/2–1787), politician', *ODNB*, 23 Sept. 2004 [https://doi.org/10.1093/ref:odnb/14546, accessed 23 February 2020]

Cox, Gary W., 'War, moral hazard and ministerial responsibility: England after the Glorious Revolution', *Journal of Economic History*, 71 (2011) pp. 133–61

Cullen, L. M., 'Landlords, bankers and merchants: the early Irish banking world, 1700–1820', *Hermathena*, 135 (1983) pp. 25–44
———., 'The Scottish exchange on London, 1673–1778', in S.J. Connolly, R.A. Houston, and R.J. Morris (eds.), *Conflict, identity and economic development: Ireland and Scotland, 1600–1939* (Preston: Carnegie Publishing, 1995) pp. 29–44
Davis, Andrew McFarland, 'A Connecticut land bank of the eighteenth century', *Quarterly Journal of Economics*, 13 (1898) pp. 70–84
———, 'The merchants' notes of 1733', *Proceedings of the Massachusetts Historical Society*, 17/37 (1903) pp. 184–208
Desan, Christine, *Making money: coin, currency, and the coming of capitalism* (Oxford: Oxford University Press, (2014)
Devine, T. M., *The tobacco lords: a study of the tobacco merchants of Glasgow and their trading activities, c. 1740–90* (Edinburgh: Edinburgh University Press, 1990)
Dickson, P.G.M., *The financial revolution in England: a study in the development of public credit, 1688–1756* (London: Macmillan, 1967)
Donoughue, Bernard, *British Politics and the American Revolution: the path to war, 1773–75* (New York: St Martin's Press, 1964)
Dudley, Rowena, 'The failure of Burton's Bank and its aftermath', *Irish Economic and Social History*, 40 (2013) pp. 1–30
Dull, Jonathan, *The miracle of American independence: twenty ways things could have turned out differently* (Lincoln, NE: Potomac Books and University of Nebraska Press, 2015)
Dunn, Elizabeth E., '"Grasping at the shadow": the Massachusetts currency debate, 1690–1751', *New England Quarterly*, 71 (1998) pp. 54–76
Edelson, S. Max, *The new map of empire: how Britain imagined America before independence* (Cambridge, MA: Harvard University Press, 2017)
Edling, Max M., *A Hercules in the cradle: war, money, and the American state, 1783–1867* (Chicago, IL: University of Chicago Press, 2014)
Edwards, Andrew Edward, 'Grenville's silver hammer: the problem of money in the Stamp Act Crisis', *Journal of American History*, 104 (2017) pp. 337–62
Ernst, Joseph Albert, *Money and politics in America, 1755–1775: a study in the Currency Act of 1764 and the political economy of revolution* (Chapel Hill, NC: University of North Carolina Press, 1973)
Ferguson, E. James, 'Currency finance: an interpretation of colonial monetary practices', *William and Mary Quarterly*, 10 (1953) pp. 153–80
———, *The power of the purse: a history of American public finance, 1776–1790* (Chapel Hill: University of North Carolina Press, 1961)
Ferguson, Niall, 'Introduction. Virtual History: towards a 'chaotic' theory of the past', in Niall Ferguson (ed.), *Virtual History: alternatives and counterfactuals* (London: Pan, 2003) pp. 1–90

Fetter, Frank Whitson, *Development of British monetary orthodoxy, 1797–1875* (Fairfield, NJ: A.M. Kelley, 1965)
Fox, David, 'The Anglo-Scots monetary union of 1707', *Edinburgh Law Review*, 23 (2019) pp. 360–87
Freiberg, Malcolm, 'Thomas Hutchinson and the provincial currency', *New England Quarterly*, 30 (1957) pp. 190–208
Gipson, Lawrence, *The British Empire before the American Revolution* (15 vols., Caldwell, ID and New York: Caxton Printers and Knopf, 1936–70)
Goldberg, Dror, 'Why was America's first bank aborted?', *Journal of Economic History*, 71 (2011) pp. 211–22
Goodwin, Gordon, and Carter, Philip, 'Cuming, Sir Alexander, second baronet (1691–1775)', *ODNB* [https://doi.org/10.1093/ref:odnb/6891, accessed 23 Feb. 2020]
Goodspeed, Tyler Beck, *Legislating instability: Adam Smith, free banking, and the financial crisis of 1772* (Cambridge, MA: Harvard University Press, 2016)
Goslinga, Cornelis Ch and Yperen, Maria J. L. van, *The Dutch in the Caribbean and in the Guianas, 1680–1791* (Assen/Maastricht: Van Gorcum, 1985)
Graham, Aaron, 'Corruption and contractors in the North Atlantic, 1754–63', *English Historical Review*, 133 (2018) pp. 1093–1119
———, 'Credit, confidence and the circulation of Exchequer bills in the early financial revolution', *Financial History Review*, 26 (2019) pp. 63–80
Greene, Jack P., 'Martin Bladen's blueprint for a colonial union', *William and Mary Quarterly*, 17 (1960) pp. 516–30
———., '"A dress of horror": Henry McCulloh's objections to the Stamp Act', *Huntington Library Quarterly*, 26 (1963) pp. 253–62
Greene, Jack P. and Jellison, Richard M., 'The Currency Act of 1764 in imperial-colonial relations, 1764–1776', *William and Mary Quarterly*, 18 (1961) pp. 485–518
Griffin, Patrick, *The Townshend moment: the making of empire and revolution in the eighteenth century* (New Haven, CT: Harvard University Press, 2018)
Grubb, Farley, 'Creating the U.S. dollar currency union 1748–1811; a quest for monetary stability or a usurpation of state sovereignty for personal gain?', *American Economic Review*, 93 (2003) pp. 1778–98
———, 'Is paper money just paper money? Experimentation and variation in the paper monies issued by the American colonies from 1690 to 1775', *Research in Economic History*, 32 (2016) pp. 147–224
Guttridge, G.H., 'Thomas Pownall's *The Administration of the Colonies*: the six editions', *William and Mary Quarterly*, 26 (1969) pp. 31–46
Gwyn, Julian, *The enterprising admiral: the personal fortune of Admiral Sir Peter Warren* (Montreal: McGill-Queen's University Press, 1974)
———, 'The impact of British military spending on the colonial money markets, 1760–1783', *Historical Papers/Communications Historiques*, 15/1 (1980) pp. 77–99

Hamilton, H., 'Scotland's balance of payments problem in 1762', *Economic History Review*, 5 (1953) pp. 344–57

Hammond, Bray, *Banks and politics in America: from the Revolution to the Civil War* (Princeton, NJ: Princeton University Press, 1957)

Hendrickson, Jill M., *Regulation and instability in U.S. commercial banking: a history of crises* (Basingstoke and New York: Palgrave Macmillan, 2011)

Hinderaker, Eric, *Elusive empires: constructing colonialism in the Ohio Valley, 1673–1800* (Cambridge: Cambridge University Press, 1997)

Hofstra, Warren R., *The planting of New Virginia: settlement and landscape in the Shenandoah Valley* (Baltimore, MD: Johns Hopkins University Press, 2004)

Hoppit, Julian, 'The landed interest and the national interest, 1660–1800', in Julian Hoppit (ed.), *Parliaments, nations and identities in Britain and Ireland, 1660–1850* (Manchester: Manchester University Press, 2003) pp. 83–102

Horsefield, John Keith, *British monetary experiments, 1650–1710* (London: G. Bell & Sons, 1960)

———, 'The origins of Blackwell's *Model* of a bank', *William and Mary Quarterly*, 23 (1966) pp. 121–35

Houston, Alan Craig, *Benjamin Franklin and the politics of improvement* (New Haven and London: Yale University Press, 2008)

Ingersoll, Thomas N., *The Loyalist problem in revolutionary New England* (Cambridge: Cambridge University Press, 2017)

Ito, Seiichiro, 'The making of institutional credit in England, 1600 to 1688', *European Journal of the History of Economic Thought*, 18 (2011) pp. 487–519

Johnson, Allen S., 'The passage of the Sugar Act', *William and Mary Quarterly*, 16 (1959) pp. 507–14

Jones, Geoffrey, *British multinational banking, 1830–1990* (Oxford: Oxford University Press, 1993)

Kelly, Patrick Hyde, 'Berkeley and the idea of a national bank', *Eighteenth-century Ireland/Iris an dá chultúr*, 25 (2010) pp. 98–117

Kemmerer, Donald L., 'The colonial loan-office system in New Jersey', *Journal of Political Economy*, 47 (1939) pp. 867–74

Kerridge, Eric, *Trade and banking in early modern England* (Manchester: Manchester University Press, 1988)

King, W.T.C., *History of the London discount market* (London: F. Cass, 1972)

Kinkel, Sarah, *Disciplining the empire: politics, governance, and the rise of the British navy* (Cambridge, MA: Harvard University Press, 2018)

Kleer, Richard, '"Fictitious Cash": English public finances and paper money, 1689–97', in Charles McGrath and Christopher Fauske (eds.), *Money, power and print: interdisciplinary studies on the financial revolution in the British Isles* (Newark, DE: University of Delaware Press, 2008) pp. 70–103

———, '"A new species of money": British Exchequer bills, 1707–1711', *Financial History Review*, 22 (2015) pp. 179–203

———, *Money, politics and power: banking and public finance in wartime England, 1694–1696* (London: Routledge, 2017)
Kosmetatos, Paul, *The 1772–73 British credit crisis* (London: Palgrave Macmillan, 2018)
Kulikoff, Allan, *From British peasants to colonial American farmers* (Chapel Hill, NC and London: University of North Carolina Press, 2000)
———, 'Benjamin Franklin and the theater of empire', *Pennsylvania Magazine of History and Biography*, 141 (2017) pp. 77–90
Legg, Marie-Louise, 'Money and reputations: the effects of the banking crises of 1755 and 1760', *Eighteenth-century Ireland/Iris an dá chultúr*, 11 (1996) pp. 74–87
Leighton-Boyce, J.A.S.L., *Smiths the bankers: 1658–1958* (London: National Provincial bank, 1958)
Lester, Richard A., 'Currency issues to overcome depressions in Pennsylvania, 1723 and 1729', *Journal of Political Economy*, 46 (1938) pp. 324–75
Maier, Pauline, *From resistance to revolution: colonial radicals and the development of American opposition to Britain, 1765–1776* (New York: Knopf, 1972)
Marshall, P. J., 'Empire and authority in the later eighteenth century', *Journal of Imperial and Commonwealth History*, 15 (1987) pp. 105–22
———., *The making and unmaking of empires: Britain, India, and America c.1750–1783* (Oxford: Oxford University Press, 2005)
———., 'Macleane, Lauchlin [*formerly* Laughlin McLean] (1728/9–1778)', *ODNB* [https://doi.org/10.1093/ref:odnb/40597, accessed 23 Feb. 2020]
Martin, Alfred S., 'The King's Customs: Philadelphia, 1763–1774', *William and Mary Quarterly*, 5 (1948) pp. 201–16
Martin, David A., 'The changing role of foreign money in the United States, 1782–1857', *Journal of Economic History*, 37 (1977) pp. 1009–27
McCallum, Bennett T., 'Money and prices in colonial America: a new test of competing theories', *Journal of Political Economy*, 100 (1992) pp. 143–61
McCleskey, Turk and Squire, James C., 'Pennsylvania credit in the Virginia backcountry, 1746–1755', *Pennsylvania History*, 81 (2014) pp. 207–25
McCullough, A. B., *Money and exchange in Canada to 1900* (Toronto: Dundurn Press, 1984) 323 p
McCurry, Allan J., 'The North Government and the outbreak of the American Revolution', *Huntington Library Quarterly*, 34 (1971) pp. 141–57
McCusker, John J., *Money and exchange in Europe and America, 1600–1775: a handbook* (London: Macmillan, 1978)
———., 'Colonial civil servant and counter-revolutionary: Thomas Irving (1738?–1800) in Boston, Charleston and London', in John J. McCusker (ed.), *Essays in the economic history of the Atlantic world* (London: Routledge, 1997) pp. 190–221

McCusker, John J. and Menard, Russell R., *The economy of British America, 1607–1789* (Chapel Hill, NC: Published for the Institute of Early American History and Culture by the University of North Carolina Press, 1991)

McGilvary, George K., *Guardian of the East India Company: the life of Laurence Sulivan* (London: I.B. Tauris, 2005)

———., *East India patronage and the British state: the Scottish elite and politics in the eighteenth century* (London: Tauris Academic Studies, 2008)

Melton, Frank T., *Sir Robert Clayton and the origins of English deposit banking, 1658–1685* (Cambridge: Cambridge University Press, 1986)

Michener, Ronald, 'Fixed exchange rates and the quantity theory in colonial America', *Carnegie-Rochester Conference Series on Public Policy*, 27 (1987) pp. 233–308

———, 'Redemption theories and the value of American colonial paper money', *Financial History Review*, 22 (2016) pp. 315–35

Michener, Ronald and Wright, Robert E., 'State "currencies" and the transition to the U.S. Dollar: clarifying some conclusions', *American Economic Review*, 95 (2005) pp. 682–703

———, 'Development of the US monetary union', *Financial History Review*, 13 (2006) pp. 19–41

Middleton, Simon, 'Private credit in eighteenth-century New York City: the Mayor's Court Papers, 1681–1776', *Journal of Early American History*, 2 (2012) pp. 150–77

Mints, Lloyd W., *A history of banking theory in Great Britain and the United States* (Chicago: University of Chicago Press, 1945)

Moore, Katie A., 'America's first economic stimulus package: paper money and the body politic in colonial Pennsylvania, 1715–1730', *Pennsylvania History*, 83 (2016) pp. 529–57

———., 'The blood that nourishes the body politic: the origins of paper money in early America', *Early American Studies*, 17 (2019) pp. 1–36

Muldrew, Craig, 'Wages and the problem of monetary scarcity in early modern England', in Jan Lucassen (ed.), *Wages and currency: global comparisons from antiquity to the twentieth century* (Berne: Peter Lang, 2007) pp. 392–409

Mulford, Carla, *Benjamin Franklin and the Ends of Empire* (Oxford: Oxford University Press, 2015)

Mullett, Charles F., 'English imperial thinking, 1764–1783', *Political Science Quarterly*, 45 (1930) pp. 548–79

Munger, Donna Bingham, *Pennsylvania land records: a history and guide for research* (Wilmington, DE: Scholarly Resources, 1991)

Munn, C. W., 'Banking on branches: the origins and development of branch banking in the United Kingdom', in P.L Cottrell, Alice Teichova, and Takeshi Yuzawa (eds.), *Finance in the age of the corporate economy* (Aldershot: Ashgate, 1997) pp. 37–51

Munn, C.W., *The Scottish provincial banking companies 1747–1864* (Edinburgh: John Donald, 1981)

Murdoch, D.H., 'Land policy in the eighteenth-century British empire: the sale of crown lands in the Ceded Islands, 1763–1783', *Historical Journal*, 27 (1984) pp. 549–74

Murray, Atholl L., 'The Scottish recoinage of 1707–9 and its aftermath', *British Numismatic Journal*, 72 (2003) pp. 115–34

Namier, L. B. and Brooke, John L. (eds.), *History of Parliament: the House of Commons, 1754–1790* (3 vols., London: Published by Her Majesty's Stationery Office for the History of Parliament Trust, 1964)

Narsey, Wadan, *British Imperialism and the making of colonial currency systems* (London: Palgrave Macmillan, 2016) xv, 356 pages

Nettels, Curtis P., *The money supply of the American colonies before 1720* (Madison, WI: University of Wisconsin Press, 1934)

Newell, Margaret Ellen, *From dependency to independence: economic revolution in colonial New England* (Ithaca, NY and London: Cornell University Press, 1998)

Norris, John, *Shelburne and reform* (London: Macmillan, 1963)

North, D. C. and Weingast, B. R., 'Constitutions and commitment: the evolution of institutions governing public choice in 17th century England', *Journal of Economic History*, 49 (1989) pp. 803–832

Novak, William J., 'The myth of the "weak" American state', *American Historical Review*, 113 (2008) pp. 752–72

O'Brien, Patrick, 'The political economy of British taxation, 1660–1815', *Economic History Review, 2nd ser*, 41 (1988) pp. 1–32

O'Brien, Patrick and Palma, Nuno, 'Danger to the Old Lady of Threadneedle Street? The Bank Restriction Act and the regime shift to paper money, 1797–1821', *European Review of Economic History*, 24 (2020) pp. 390–426

O'Shaughnessy, Andrew, *An empire divided: the American Revolution and the British Caribbean* (Philadelphia: University of Pennsylvania Press, 2000)

Ollerenshaw, Philip, *Banking in nineteenth-century Ireland: the Belfast banks, 1825–1914* (Manchester: Manchester University Press, 1987)

Pargellis, Stanley McCrory, *Lord Loudoun in North America* (New Haven, CT: Yale University Press, 1933)

Pearce, Adrian John, *British trade with Spanish America, 1763–1808* (Liverpool: Liverpool University Press, 2007)

Perkins, Edwin J., 'Conflicting views on fiat currency: Britain and its North American colonies in the eighteenth century', *Business History*, 33 (1991) pp. 8–30

———., *American public finance and financial services, 1700–1815* (Columbus, OH: Ohio State University Press, 1994)

Plummer, Wilbur C., 'Consumer credit in Philadelphia', *The Pennsylvania Magazine of History and Biography*, 66 (1942) pp. 385–409

Pressnell, L. S., *Country banking in the industrial revolution* (Oxford: Clarendon Press, 1956)

Preston, David L., *Braddock's Defeat: the Battle of the Monongahela and the road to revolution* (Oxford: Oxford University Press, 2015)

Price, Jacob M., 'The money question', *Reviews in American History*, 2 (1974) pp. 364–73

———., *Capital and credit in British overseas trade: the view from the Chesapeake, 1700–1776* (Cambridge, MA: Harvard University Press, 1980)

———., 'The Bank of England's discount activity and the merchants of London, 1694–1773', in Ian Blanchard, et al. (eds.), *Industry and finance in early modern history* (Stuttgart: Franz Steiner, 1992) pp. 92–115

Purvis, Thomas L., *Proprietors, patronage, and paper money: legislative politics in New Jersey, 1703–1776* (New Brunswick, N.J.; London: Rutgers University Press, 1986)

Quintanilla, Mark, 'Mercantile communities in the Ceded Islands: the Alexander Bartlet & George Campbell Company', *International Social Science Review*, 79 (2004) pp. 14–26

Rabushka, Alvin, *Taxation in colonial America* (Princeton: Princeton University Press, 2008)

Rao, Gautham, *National duties: custom houses and the making of the American state* (Chicago, IL: University of Chicago Press, 2016)

———, 'The new historiography of the early Federal government: institutions, contexts and the imperial state', *William and Mary Quarterly*, 77 (2020) pp. 97–128

Remer, Rosalind, 'Old Lights and New Money: a note on religion, economics and the social order in 1740 Boston', *William and Mary Quarterly*, 47 (1990) pp. 466–73

Rice, Geoffrey W., 'British foreign policy and the Falkland Islands crisis of 1770–1', *International History Review*, 32 (2010) pp. 273–305

Richter, Daniel K., 'Native Americans, the Plan of 1764 and a British Empire that never was', in Alan Tully and Robert Olwell (eds.), *Cultures and identities in colonial British America* (Baltimore, MD: John Hopkins University Press, 2005) pp. 269–92

Robson, Robert, *The attorney in eighteenth-century England* (Cambridge: Cambridge University Press, 1959)

Rogers, Alan, *Empire and liberty: American resistance to British authority, 1755–1763* (Berkeley: University of California Press, 1974)

Roney, Jessica C., *Governed by a spirit of opposition: the origins of American political practice in colonial Philadelphia* (Baltimore, MD: Johns Hopkins University Press, 2014)

Rubini, Dennis, 'Politics and the battle for the banks, 1688–1697', *English Historical Review*, 85 (1970) pp. 693–714

Russell, Mattie, 'McCulloh, Henry', in William Powell (ed.), *Dictionary of North Carolina Biography* (6 vols, Chapel Hill, NC: Columbia University Press, 1979–2001) vol. iv, 133

Ryder, M., 'The Bank of Ireland, 1721: land, credit and dependency', *Historical Journal*, 25 (1982) pp. 557–82

Sachs, William S., 'Interurban correspondents and the development of a national economy before the Revolution: New York as a case study', *New York History*, 36 (1955) pp. 320–35

Saville, Richard, *Bank of Scotland: a history, 1695–1995* (Edinburgh: Edinburgh University Press, 1996)

Schutz, John A., *Thomas Pownall: British defender of American liberty. A study of Anglo-American relations in the Eighteenth century* (Glendale, CA: Arthur H. Clark, 1951)

Schweitzer, Mary M., *Custom and contract: household, government, and the economy in colonial Pennsylvania* (New York and Guildford: Columbia University Press, 1987)

———., 'State-issued currency and the ratification of the U.S. Constitution', *Journal of Economic History*, 49 (1989) pp. 311–22

Scott, Jonathon, '"Good Night Amsterdam": Sir George Downing and Anglo-Dutch statebuilding', *English Historical Review*, 118 (2003) pp. 334–56

Shannon, H.A., 'Evolution of the colonial sterling exchange standard', *Staff Papers (International Monetary Fund)*, 1 (1950–1) pp. 334–54

Shannon, Timothy J., *Indians and colonists at the crossroads of empire: the Albany Congress of 1754* (Ithaca, NY: Cornell University Press, 2000)

Shepherd, James F. and Williamson, Samuel H., 'The coastal trade of the British North American colonies, 1768–1772', *Journal of Economic History*, 32 (1972) pp. 783–810

Sheridan, Richard B., 'The Molasses Act and the market strategy of the British sugar planters', *Journal of Economic History*, 17 (1957) pp. 62–83

———., 'The British credit crisis of 1772 and the American colonies', *Journal of Economic History*, 20 (1960) pp. 161–86

———., *Sugar and slavery: an economic history of the British West Indies, 1623–1775* (Barbados: Caribbean University Press, 1974) xiii, 529 p.

Shy, John W., *Toward Lexington: the role of the British Army in the coming of the American Revolution* (Princeton, NJ: Princeton University Press, 1965) x, 463 p.

Sklansky, Jeffrey, *Sovereign of the market: The money question in early America* (Chicago: University of Chicago Press, 2017)

Slack, Paul, *The invention of improvement: information and material progress in seventeenth-century England* (Oxford: Oxford University Press, 2015)

Smith, Bruce D., 'American colonial monetary regimes: the failure of the quantity theory and some evidence in favour of an alternate view', *Canadian Journal of Economics/Revue canadienne d'Economique*, 18 (1985) pp. 531–65

Smith, S. D., 'Merchants and planters revisited', *Economic History Review*, 55 (2002) pp. 434–65

———., *Slavery, family, and gentry capitalism in the British Atlantic: the world of the Lascelles, 1648–1834* (Cambridge; New York: Cambridge University Press, 2006)

Smoak, Katherine, 'The weight of necessity: counterfeit coins in the British Atlantic world, circa 1760–1800', *William and Mary Quarterly*, 74 (2017) pp. 467–502

Sobel, Robert, *For want of a nail: if Burgoyne had won at Saratoga* (London: Greenhill, February 1997)

Soltow, James H., 'The role of Williamsburg in the Virginia economy, 1750–1775', *William and Mary Quarterly*, 15 (1958) pp. 467–82

———., 'Scottish traders in Virginia, 1750–1775', *Economic History Review*, 12 (1959) pp. 83–98

Sosin, Jack M., *Whitehall and the wilderness: the Middle West in British colonial policy, 1760–1775* (Lincoln, NE: University of Nebraska Press, 1961)

———., 'Imperial regulation of colonial paper money, 1764–1773', *Pennsylvania Magazine of History and Biography*, 87 (1964) pp. 174–86

Stark, Bruce P., 'The New London Society and Connecticut politics, 1732–1740', *Connecticut History Review*, 25 (1984) pp. 1–21

Stasavage, David, 'Partisan politics and public debt: the importance of the 'Whig Supremacy' for Britain's financial revolution', *European Review of Economic History*, 11 (2007) pp. 123–53

Steele, Ian K., *Politics of colonial policy: the Board of Trade in colonial administration 1696–1720* (Oxford: Clarendon Press, 1968)

Stout, Neil R., *The Royal Navy in America, 1760–1775: a study of enforcement of British colonial policy in the era of the American Revolution* (Annapolis, MD: Naval Institute Press, 1973)

Sumner, Scott, 'Colonial currency and the quantity theory of money: a critique of Smith's interpretation', *Journal of Economic History*, 53 (1993) pp. 139–45

Sussman, Nathan and Yafeh, Yishay, 'Institutional reforms, financial development and sovereign debt: Britain, 1690–1790', *Journal of Economic History*, 66/4 (2006) pp. 906–35

Sutherland, Lucy, 'Sir George Colebrooke's world corner in alum, 1771–73', *Economic Journal*, 46 (1936) pp. 237–58

Sutherland, Lucy Stuart, *The East India Company in eighteenth-century politics* (Oxford: Clarendon Press, 1962)

Temin, Peter and Voth, Hans-Joachim, *Prometheus shackled: goldsmith banks and England's financial revolution* (Oxford: Oxford University Press, 2013)

Thayer, Theodore, 'The Land-Bank system in the American colonies', *Journal of Economic History*, 13 (1953) pp. 145–59
Thomas, P. D. G, *The Townshend duties crisis: the second phase of the American Revolution, 1767–1773* (Oxford: Clarendon Press, 1987)
———, *Tea party to independence: the third phase of the American Revolution 1773–1776* (Oxford: Clarendon Press, 1991)
Tiedemann, Joseph S., 'Interconnected communities: the middle colonies on the eve of the American Revolution', *Pennsylvania History*, 71 (2009) pp. 1–41
Tracy, Nicholas, 'The Falkland Islands crisis of 1770; use of naval force', *English Historical Review*, 40 (1975) pp. 40–75
Truxes, Thomas M., *Defying empire: trading with the enemy in colonial New York* (New Haven, CT: Yale University Press, 2008)
Ubbelohde, Carl, *The Vice-Admiralty Courts and the American Revolution* (Chapel Hill: Published for the Institute of Early American History and Culture by the University of North Carolina Press, 1960)
Vickers, Douglas, *Studies in the Theory of Money, 1690–1776* (London: Peter Owen, 1960)
Walsh, Patrick, *The South Sea bubble and Ireland: money, banking and investment, 1690–1721* (London: Boydell & Brewer, 2014)
Watson, Alan D., 'A letter of Charles Williamos to Lord Dartmouth, July 1766', *South Carolina Historical Magazine*, 77 (1976a) pp. 1–9
———., 'The quitrent system in royal South Carolina', *William and Mary Quarterly*, 33 (1976b) pp. 183–211
Webb, Stephen Saunders, 'William Blathwayt, Imperial Fixer: from Popish Plot to Glorious Revolution (pt. i)', *William and Mary Quarterly*, 3rd ser, 25 (1968) pp. 4–21
———, 'William Blathwayt, Imperial Fixer: muddling through to empire, 1689–1717 (pt. ii)', *William and Mary Quarterly*, 3rd ser, 26 (1969) pp. 373–415
Weiss, Roger W., 'The issue of paper money in the American colonies, 1720–1774', *Journal of Economic History*, 30 (1970) pp. 770–84
Wells, John and Willis, Douglas, 'Revolution, restoration and debt repudiation: the Jacobite threat to England's institutions and economic growth', *Journal of Economic History*, 60 (2000) pp. 418–41
Wennerlind, Carl, *Casualties of credit: the English financial revolution, 1620–1720* (Cambridge, MA: Harvard University Press, 2011)
West, Robert Craig, 'Money in the colonial American economy', *Economic Inquiry*, 16 (1978) pp. 1–15
White, Richard, *The middle ground: Indians, empires, and republics in the Great Lakes region, 1650–1815* (Cambridge: Cambridge University Press, 2011)
Wicker, Elmus, 'Colonial monetary standards contrasted: evidence from the Seven Years War', *Journal of Economic History*, xlv (1985) pp. 869–84

Wood, John H., *A history of central banking in Great Britain and the United States* (Cambridge: Cambridge University Press, 2005)

Wright, Robert E., *Origins of commercial banking in America, 1750–1800* (Lanham, MD: Rowman & Littlefield, 2001)

Yirush, Craig, *Settlers, liberty, and empire: the roots of early American political theory, 1675–1775* (Cambridge: Cambridge University Press, 2011)

Index[1]

A

American Revolution, 14–15, 85–88
  See also Empire, and American Revolution
Amherst, Sir Jeffrey, 82
Army sterling, *see* Empire, and warfare, military finance
Australia, 11, 16, 92

B

Bank of England, 13, 28, 30, 47–49, 57, 58, 61, 64, 65, 81–83, 88, 90, 91, 95n26
Bank of Ireland, 14
Bank of North America, 77, 88, 89
Bank of Scotland, 48, 65, 91
Bank of the United States, 16, 89
Banks, by name
  Amsterdam Wisselbank, 14
  Ayr Bank, 29, 31, 49
  Bank of America, 61, 64, 88
  Bank of Philadelphia, 56–58
  Company of Merchants trading in Exchanges, 64–67
  General Loan Office, 27, 29, 32–34, 42, 45n25, 57–58, 80
  Land Bank, Massachusetts, 15, 29, 50–51
  National Land Bank, 28–29, 31
  Royal Bank, 52–55
  Royal Provincial Bank, 54, 55
  Silver Bank, Massachusetts, 15, 50–51
  See also Bank of England; Bank of Ireland; Bank of North America; Bank of Scotland; Bank of the United States; British Linen Bank; Royal Bank of Scotland

---

[1] Note: Page numbers followed by 'n' refer to notes.

Banks, by place
  Barbados, 29
  Charleston, 51–53
  colonial, 66, 92
  England, 13, 14, 28–31, 47–51,
    56–58, 60–61, 65–66,
    82, 85, 90
  Ireland, 3, 14, 90
  Jamaica, 51, 53
  Maryland, 30, 32
  Massachusetts, 15, 29, 50–51
  Philadelphia, 31–34, 51, 56–58, 88
  Scotland, 5–6, 32–34, 48–51, 58,
    65–66, 90, 91
  United States, 16, 88–90
Banks, by type
  Goldsmith-banks, 48–49, 56, 58
  Joint-stock banks, 16, 29, 48–52,
    57–58, 64–66, 88–90
  land banks, 3, 15, 48–52, 56–58,
    61, 63–67, 79, 80
  private or 'country' banks, 3,
    16, 30, 90
  Scotch system, 7, 49, 64–67
  Scrivener-banks, 28, 45n30
  'specie' banks, 12, 29–31,
    47–58, 64–67, 81–83, 87,
    89, 90, 92
Banks, management
  branches, 32, 41, 61, 64–66
  Court of Directors, 36–38, 61,
    64, 66–67
  land valuation (*see* Land)
  professional staff, 32–34, 36–38,
    42, 51, 66
  profits, 30, 32, 34, 37, 42,
    55–57, 61, 80
  specie reserves, 30, 47–48, 51,
    56–58, 61, 92
Banks, regulation, 5–6, 16, 26–34,
  36–38, 41–42, 47–50, 60–61,
  65–66, 88–93

'Bubble Act' 1741, 13, 57
Scottish Banking Act
  1765, 5–6
See also Money, regulation
Barbados, 29, 41
Barré, Isaac, 39
Board of Trade, 8, 29, 35, 58–60,
  78, 79, 92
See also Empire, and ambitions
British Guiana, 92
British Linen Bank, 48, 65
Burke, Edmund, 39

C
Canada, 7, 8, 10, 16, 37, 39, 41, 50,
  78, 91–92
  Montreal, 39
  Quebec, 85
Cape of Good Hope, 92
Caribbean, 2, 4, 7, 8, 10, 23n50, 41,
  78, 86, 91–93
'Ceded Islands,' 7–9, 39, 40,
  73n74, 78
Coin, *see* Money, coin
Colebrooke, Sir George, 46n47
Connecticut, 70n24
Cuming, Sir Alexander
  currency proposals, 51–59,
    67, 78
  views of empire, 53–56, 59
Currency, *see* Money

D
Dartmouth, earl of, William Legge,
  35, 36, 85, 86
Dollars (Spanish America), 4, 9–11,
  32, 39, 41, 52, 83
Dollars (United States), 15–16,
  88–90, 92
Dominica, *see* 'Ceded Islands'

E

East India Company (British), 39, 92
East India Company (Dutch), 67
East Indies, 16, 92
Edelson, Max, 7, 8, 78
Empire, and ambitions, 29, 54–56
   after 1764, 6–9, 15–16, 31–32,
     35–36, 38, 40, 79, 90
   Albany Plan (1754), 7, 31, 35, 79
   before 1764, 7, 11–14, 53–56, 58–64
   Dominion of New England
     (1686), 7, 29
Empire, and American Revolution, 11,
   14, 87–89
   and hypotheticals, 81–86
Empire, and commerce, 2–4, 7–9, 12,
   36, 40, 52–53, 57, 61, 78–80
   and ambitions, 7, 12, 15, 34,
     36–38, 40–41, 55–56, 59,
     66–67, 79
   and intercolonial trade, 8–10, 41, 79
   See also Empire, and revenue, Sugar
     Act (1764)
Empire, and money, *see* Money;
   Proposals; Banks
Empire, and Native Americans, 7–8,
   21n28, 55, 62
Empire, and revenue, 7–8, 11–12, 30,
   34, 40, 50, 52–55, 59–63,
   82, 84, 89
   and ambitions, 8, 34, 37, 40,
     53, 63, 93
   Stamp Act (1764), 7, 11–12, 40,
     53, 59–63, 73n74
   Sugar Act (1764), 8, 59, 60, 62, 63, 79
Empire, and slavery, 3–5, 8, 53
Empire, and warfare, 7–8, 34, 39, 53,
   60–63, 81–86
   and ambitions, 7–8, 35, 37,
     60–62, 78, 81
   military finance, 9–12, 14, 15, 34,
     37, 80–84, 87–92, 94n7

Ernst, Joseph, 5, 13, 16n1, 63, 79
Exchequer Bills, *see* Money, paper,
   Exchequer bills
Exchequer Bills of Union, *see*
   Proposals, by Henry McCulloh
Exchequer Orders, 49–50

F

Falkland Islands Crisis (1770),
   96n34
Ferguson, James, 3, 87, 88
Finance, crises of
   of 1763, 4, 40
   of 1772, 4, 31, 49, 84
Finance, private
   and banking (*see* Banks, by type)
   in Britain, 2–6, 8, 28–29, 40,
     47–50, 52, 78, 81,
     83–86, 90, 91
   colonial indebtedness and imperial
     dependency, 36, 38, 42,
     53–55, 58, 59
   in colonies, 2–6, 8–9, 29–32, 38,
     49–53, 79, 83, 84, 87,
     88, 91, 92
   in the United States, 89–90
   See also Banks; Money; Proposals
Finance, public
   in Britain, 14–16, 28–29, 48–50,
     83–85, 89, 91
   in colonies, 29–31, 34, 37, 42,
     47–51, 91–93
   in the United States, 87–90
Floridas, 7, 8, 37, 41, 78
Franklin, Benjamin
   currency proposals, 31–34, 36–38,
     42, 58, 64, 79–81
   currency reforms, 31–35, 58,
     63–64, 67, 79
   views of empire, 7, 28, 31,
     32, 35, 79

G
Gage, Thomas, 85, 86
Georgia, 8
Grenville, George, 32, 53, 62, 64
Grubb, Farley, 5, 88

H
Halifax, earl of, George Montagu-Dunk, 72n57, 73n74
Hamilton, Alexander, 84, 88
Hertford, earl of, Francis Seymour-Conway, 38
Hillsborough, earl of, Wills Hill, 79

I
Illinois, 7, 8, 10

J
Jackson, Henry, 31, 56–58, 61, 88
Jamaica, 8, 41, 92

L
Land
  as basis for banking (*see* Banks, by type; Land banks)
  and improvement, 3–4, 8–9, 28–30, 35, 38, 40–43, 53
  registries, 30
  valuation, 29, 33, 36
Land banks, 27–43
Law, John, 53, 56
Little, Otis, 54, 63

M
Macleane, Lachlan, 38–43, 61, 74n86
Manchester, duke of, George Montagu, 35
Martinique, 39
Maryland, 3, 30, 32, 40, 41
Massachusetts, 3, 13, 15, 29, 32, 41, 50, 54
McCulloh, Henry, 81, 82, 86–88
  currency proposals, 58–64
  views of empire, 58–60
Military finance, *see* Empire, and warfare, military finance
Monetary unions, *see* Money, and monetary unions
Money, and monetary unions, 1–3, 14–16, 78, 87–93
Money, by place
  Britain, 13
  Caribbean, 2, 8, 10, 16, 29, 41, 51, 93
  colonial America, 2–6, 9–14, 31–32, 35, 39–42, 50–65, 79–84
  elsewhere, 11, 16, 81, 91
  England, 13, 14, 28–31, 47–50, 57, 66, 90–91
  Ireland, 14, 90–91
  Scotland, 5–6, 29–30, 48–51, 65–66, 90–91
  United States, 14–16, 87–90
Money, coin
  gold, 3, 4, 8, 11, 14, 15, 41, 47–49, 52, 54–57, 64, 81, 83, 90, 91
  ratings, 10–13, 15, 32, 39, 41, 48, 52, 89, 92
  shortage of, 2–4, 8, 10–13, 35–36, 48–49, 51, 56–58, 62, 81–82, 84
  silver, 3, 4, 8, 11–13, 36, 41, 47–52, 54–57, 64, 81, 83, 87, 90–92
  small change, 36, 51
  as tokens, 49, 63, 91
Money, paper, 79, 80, 82–84, 86–89, 92
  by the Bank of England (*see* Bank of England)

by the Bank of the United States (*see* Bank of the United States)
currency finance, 3–6, 14, 29–32, 34, 48, 50, 53, 62
and devaluation, 4–6, 12–14, 30–35, 40–41, 50–52, 54, 56, 60, 61, 87–89
Exchequer Bills, 49–50, 61, 81–83
by land banks, 3, 15, 27–43, 50, 57–59, 61, 79, 80, 88
by 'specie' banks, 3–6, 13, 14, 16, 47–58, 60–61, 64–67, 81–83, 87, 89, 90, 92
Money, policies, 15–16, 81, 83, 85
Currency Act, 1708, 12, 13, 15
Currency Act, 1751, 5, 6, 13, 15, 60, 79, 84
Currency Act, 1764, 3, 6, 13, 15, 20n24, 32, 42, 58, 62–64, 67, 79, 80, 83, 84
Currency Act, 1773, 6, 15, 79, 80
Order in Council, 1825, 11–12, 92
Proclamation, 1704, 12–13, 32
Money, proposals for, *see* Proposals
Money, regulation, 16
Money, theories of, 4–6, 12–14, 27–32, 40, 47–52, 55–57, 88–93
Alchemical, 14, 55
'Backing theory,' 4–5, 30
'Quantity theory,' 4–6, 31, 33–35, 41–42
Montagu, Lord Charles, 35
Morris, Robert, 88

N
Native Americans, *see* Empire, and Native Americans
Newcastle, duke of, Thomas Pelham-Holmes, 52, 71n27, 71n39, 73n60
New England, 4–7, 10–12, 29, 40, 51, 54–55, 60, 84, 85, 90

New Jersey, 10, 29–31
New York, 4, 5, 10, 29, 41, 61, 79, 82, 90
New York City, 4, 9, 10, 30, 36, 37, 51, 61, 85
North Carolina, 58–60, 64
Nova Scotia, 8, 9, 37, 41, 92
Halifax, 9

P
Paper money, *see* Money, paper
Pennsylvania, 4, 5, 10, 27, 29–33, 37–39, 41, 42, 57, 58, 61, 80, 82, 89
Philadelphia, 4, 10, 30, 31, 51, 57–58, 61, 70n24, 88
Pownall, William, 32–35
Proposals
by Benjamin Franklin, 31–35, 42–43
by Charles Williamos, 35–38, 42–43
by the 'Company of Merchants,' 64–67
by Henry McCulloh, 58–65, 81, 82, 86–88
by Lachlane Macleane, 38–43, 61
by Richard Jackson, 31, 56–58, 61, 88
by Sir Alexander Cuming, 53–56

R
Rhode Island, 4–6, 10, 31, 34, 88
Royal Bank of Scotland, 48

S
Saint Domingue, 8
Shelburne, earl of, William Petty, 38–39

Slavery, *see* Empire, and slavery
South Carolina, 5, 10, 29, 34, 35, 37, 38, 41, 42, 51–54, 56, 64
  Charleston, 51–52
Specie, *see* Money
St Kitts, 8
St Vincent, *see* 'Ceded Islands'

T
Townshend, Charles, 63–64
Treasury, 11, 22n39, 33–35, 37, 38, 50, 54, 61, 81, 91, 92

See also Empire, and revenue; Empire, and warfare, military finance

V
Virginia, 3, 6, 10, 41, 79, 83
  Williamsburg, 22n40, 61

W
West India Company (Dutch), 66–67
Wilkes, John, 39
Williamos, Charles, 35–38, 42–43

Lightning Source UK Ltd.
Milton Keynes UK
UKHW022051090421
381746UK00003B/83